Pennies by the Sea

The Life and Times of Joyland Amusements, Bridlington

NICK LAISTER

SKELTER
PUBLISHING

A catalogue record for this book is available from the British Library

ISBN 0-9544573-5-8
       978-0-9544573-5-8

Designed and typeset in Great Britain by Paul Barrett Book Production, Cambridge

With thanks to Justin Garvanovic

Printed by Thanet Press Ltd, Margate, Kent

To Mum and Dad

Contents

Acknowledgements

As so little has been written about Joyland, and amusement arcades in general, this book has been based almost entirely on primary research: interviews, trawls through libraries and local records, local newspapers and holiday brochures. I am therefore indebted to the many people who gave up their time to help me assemble this book.

Thanks to Joyland mechanics Walter Hoyes, Ronald Walls, Dennis Tate, Ron Stockwell and Derek Taylor, who made themselves available for long interviews and invited me into their homes. A big thank you also to Gordon Lowe, who runs the Forum website, and to Stuart Keane, who owned and operated the Joyland rides in the 1970s and 1980s. Thanks also to John Noble Jnr, one of the directors of J. Noble & Sons Ltd, the current owners of Joyland who gave me a fantastic 'behind-the-scenes tour'.

In addition, the following amusement caterers, who operate or operated other arcades in the town, all gave up their time to meet me. I would like to thank Audrey Black and Geoff Gibson of Bay View Amusements, Chris Parcell of the Sixties Coffee Bar/Old Penny Memories museum, Ian Dixon of the erstwhile Vintage Toy and Train Museum and Wes Walker of Walkers Tussauds. Thanks also to Jim Dodgson, who worked on the Joyland buildings over many years and told me many fascinating stories that have helped me to bring the Joyland story to life. Thanks also go to local estate agent, Reg Spencer, who marketed Joyland in the early 1970s and had thankfully retained a copy of his marketing material.

The Bridlington Free Press has been a great help in supplying photographs and information, and publishing my requests for assistance with the book. Thanks, in particular, to editor Selwyn Dunford and reporter John Edwards. Thanks also to local independent photographer and historian, Charlie Chinnery, who I am pleased took several photographs of Joyland throughout the last 40 years, some of which appear in the book.

I would also like to record my thanks to the staff of Bridlington Reference Library, in particular Sarah Stocks, whose enthusiasm for all aspects of Bridlington's local history helped me fill some important gaps in the later stages of research. Sarah persuaded me to hold an 'amusement arcades nostalgia evening' at the Library as part of the 2006 Bridlington Arts Festival, which was a great success.

I would also like to thank fairground historian and author, Stephen Smith, for information from the World's Fair newspaper and for recounting his investigations which led to the discovery of the Joyland Ark on a farm. Thanks also to Jack Schofield, Chairman of the Fairground Society, and fairground artist Pete Tei of Tate Décor. Thanks also to World's Fair writers Keith Hamilton, Owen Ralph and Andrew McKinley, and also to Ian Trowell of the National Fairground Archive at Sheffield University. I also wish to thank Elizabeth Ward of Great Yarmouth Library, for her help on the early history of amusement arcades.

I would also like to thank the following people for their contributions: Helen Blacker, Mark Baker, Kenneth Potts, David McMillan, Mark I'Anson, Ian Atkin, Chris Youhill, Ray Cockerham, Mick Wood, John Wardley, Adrian Padgin, Pauline Rose, Brett Johnson, Simon Pattison, Pete Williams, Martin Cooper, Kerenza Evans, Eddie Kelly, Clive Briggs, Geoffrey Brown, Priscilla Worsley, Simon Reed, David Belton, Philip Hardacre, John Jackson, Mick Sheehan, Mike Wilson, Grahame Cooper, Andrew Turner, Ray Banks, Dorothy Robson,

Gareth Jones, Carol Thompson, Paul Needham, D Green, Eileen Lenderyou, John Coates, Jonathan Plumb, Linda Brown, Paul Braithwaite, Michael Smith and Barry Norman. And a special thank you to Terry Waddington, who put me in touch with some of the key people from Joyland's history and provided me with his own memories of Joyland in the war years. Special thanks also to Dave Page, my business partner in Skelter Publishing, for his support and advice throughout this project.

I also wish to record the help given to me by the late Dora Wright, who provided so much wonderful information on the history of the Joyland site, which was owned by her husband before it became an amusement arcade. She also loaned me some truly amazing photographs. Her son-in-law, Charles Henson, was also incredibly helpful in the months following her sad passing. I hope this book can in some way be a tribute to her memory.

Finally, I would particularly like to thank Peter and Robert Brown, the grandsons of Joyland's founder, Charlotte Brown. Peter and Robert owned Joyland in the 1970s and 1980s. I enjoyed their company and listening to their fascinating stories of the arcade's history. Robert also wrote to me on numerous occasions, providing me with a huge amount of information. Both Peter and Robert also raided their family photograph albums, the result of which has been a vastly improved book. I am very grateful to them both.

Nick Laister
August 2006

Foreword by Peter Brown

This book is a credit to the author, Nick Laister. I found it to be very interesting and informative; in fact, there were several snippets that were even new to me. All in all therefore a very well researched book.

It brought back many memories of my years in Joyland – 35 in all – mostly happy ones. I am very pleased to be associated with this book, and hope that all who read it will enjoy it as much as I did.

Peter Brown
August 2006

Introduction

Joyland not only has an important place in Bridlington's history, as its biggest and most visited commercial tourist attraction, it also has a prominent place in the history of seaside amusements. It was an early example of a seaside amusement arcade, quickly becoming the largest in the country, its development showing how – through innovation and sheer determination – 'amusement caterers' (as showmen and proprietors of seaside amusement arcades are often known) overcame everything from fires to strong local objection to change the face of seaside resorts within little more than a decade. Joyland still survives to this day (although not in name), but it is a world away from the Joyland of the first half of the 20th Century.

Joyland may be an amusement arcade, but it has never been solely about slot machines. The complex also included fairground rides, bingos, cafes, zoos, more than one fun house and, in more recent years, has featured a cinema, ten pin bowling and various bars and restaurants.

Perhaps more important than the development of the buildings is the impact Joyland has had on the lives of the millions of people who visited Bridlington over the years. Many adults today remember spending long hours in the arcade and it is amazing how many people have told me they met their partners in Joyland, usually standing by the jukebox!

Joyland was not the first amusement arcade in the town, but once it started growing, its expansion seemed unstoppable. Despite the fact that amusements were first brought to the site by an engineer from Brighouse, the Joyland that would dominate Bridlington's sea front for almost 60 years was primarily developed by the Brown family, who expanded the thriving arcade by acquiring properties and bringing them into the complex. This was part of Joyland's charm, the fact that it was a mixture of different buildings from different eras, being more accident than design; even an old cinema auditorium was used in the late 1970s.

This book is the story of the Brown family's amusement empire, which expanded to include other attractions in the town. It tells of how they turned a small arcade in a former seafront shop to a palace of fun that is now widely known across Yorkshire and beyond. But it is more than just the story of an amusement arcade. It is also the first ever book about life in this most extraordinary of worlds, based on interviews with people who worked in Joyland and other arcades in the town from the 1930s to the present day. It should also therefore be of interest to social historians, as well as those who are fascinated by fairgrounds, amusement parks, arcades, slot machines and seaside holidays.

Amusement arcades are rarely in the spotlight. Local authorities invariably go to great lengths to ensure they do not appear in brochures and Bridlington was no exception. Finding good photographic material for this book was therefore extremely difficult, and became an eight-year search. But, as I hope you will agree, this book includes some fantastic images that give something of the flavour of life in this remarkable place.

ONE

Bridlington's Wonderland

"The convoluted tangle of buildings that evolved into an amusement arcade and fairground, incorporating interconnected shops, villas, old theatres, stables, sheds and yards is all part of the charm of Bridlington's seafront. Put simply, Joyland is different. Joyland is unique."

The Forum features a glittering array of slot machines across its vast floor area. This is a 1999 view of the fruit machines adjacent to the Promenade entrance. In amongst the gaming machines the Forum still includes old favourites, including the 'Grand Prix' pusher in this view. Nick Laister

Entering Bridlington's Forum leisure complex in 2006 is a very different experience from entering the complex in its previous guise as Joyland Amusements. For starters you actually have to open doors to get in. Joyland was, for most of its life, open fronted, with metal shutters that would seal the complex at night.

Whether you have entered from the seafront (Esplanade) or the town centre (Promenade) you are immediately greeted with a massive array of slot machines. No change from the Joyland of old you may think, although the slot machines are now an up-to-date mix of fruit machines and video games; but there are more fundamental differences. The concrete floors have been carpeted, the walls, which previously featured hundreds of coloured lights, are now more 'tastefully' decorated, the general appearance being sumptuous – not palatial, but certainly plush for an amusement arcade.

It is clear strolling through the building that the Forum is not an ordinary leisure complex. In fact, the use of the word 'building' is not strictly correct because, whilst the Forum is "under one roof" it is not one building. During a period of 70 years Joyland grew by acquiring surrounding property, roofing over yards and squeezing big attractions into relatively small spaces.

Nobody, at any time in Joyland's development, seems to have ever considered demolition. It would have been easy to construct a simple box with flexible space that could be used and reused over many years, but that would have missed the point. The convoluted tangle of buildings that evolved into an amusement arcade and fairground, incorporating interconnected shops, villas, old theatres, stables, sheds and yards is all part of the charm of Bridlington's seafront. Put simply, Joyland is different. Joyland is unique.

Sitting in a smartly appointed café on a raised balcony overlooking an area of gaming machines that resembles some of the big casinos on the Las Vegas strip, I recalled a tour of the complex I was given in 1999, shortly after I started researching this book. On that October day, I was taken behind the partition walls and suspended ceilings to catch a glimpse of the old Joyland.

Despite that fact that the changes that greet Forum visitors in 2006 seem significant, they are in some ways only 'skin deep'. Today's Forum is largely a stage set. The intricate collection of buildings have been made to look like an up-to-date leisure facility by creating new spaces inside the old ones. Behind all this, not only the haphazard layout of the complex remains; often actual remnants of old Joyland are still in place, hidden from view.

The old 'Super Dodgems' sign and rounding boards from the Dodgem track can still be seen above the suspended ceiling covering the bowling alley. Dodgems were a feature of Joyland for half a century. The old entrance to the Garden Café, inside the old Lounge Cinema, can still be seen behind the new three-screen cinema. The old monkey cages from the Fun House zoo are still there, and under the carpet in the American Bar, now filled with concrete, is the pit where the Waltzer once lived.

The Forum Café pictured in 1999, one of several places to eat in the new Forum.
Nick Laister

Above: Above the suspended ceiling over the Ten-Pin Bowling is this relic of old Joyland. The top of the Dodgems, with the 'Super Dodgems' sign still exists! Nick Laister

Left: Inside the old Lounge Cinema auditorium, which was brought into Joyland in 1979, are remnants of the cinema and previous Joyland attractions. In the early 1990s, the Garden Café was introduced on the site of the former Joyland Zoo. Now hidden behind new partition walls constructed to accommodate the new Forum Cinema, the old Garden Café entrance, complete with its decaying neon lighting, still exists. Nick Laister

Two

~

Before Joyland

"Ever since the growth of Bridlington as a resort in the 1880s, Yorkshire has dominated as the source of its visitors, particularly Hull, Leeds and Sheffield. Bridlington was often called 'Sheffield-on-Sea'."

A general view of Promenade before the arrival of motorised transport. Dora Wright/Charles Henson

Bridlington has always been a town of simple pleasures. Bathing brought in the first tourists in the 1700s, with visitors attracted to what they believed were the health properties of the sea.

Distinguished visitors in the town's early years included Lord Clinton and the Earl of Newcastle. They would normally stay at the turreted Fort Hall (now the site of the Leisure World swimming complex) to watch the annual horse races which took place on the sands. But perhaps Bridlington's most famous visitor was Charlotte Bronte, who saw the sea for the first time at Bridlington Bay in 1839, according to Elizabeth Gaskell's 1857 book, 'The Life of Charlotte Bronte'.

Bridlington's sea front road, Esplanade, was constructed in 1828 when it became clear that the sea was to be the town's major attraction. It was originally intended as a select public walkway, but ironically would become Bridlington's own version of Blackpool's Golden Mile, with every conceivable form of amusement on offer, from freak-shows to dodgem rides. It would, of course, also later be the location of the main entrance to Joyland.

Bridlington's evolution into a leading seaside resort was initially slow. The first notable seafront development followed the passing of an act of parliament for improving its piers and

A view of Prince's Parade under construction in c.1866 from the Victoria Rooms. The buildings in the centre of the picture front Esplanade, constructed in 1828, and would eventually become the town's largest concentration of amusement arcades.
Bridlington Library

An early photograph of Esplanade with Prince's Parade complete, showing a busy scene. The gap in the Esplanade frontage that can clearly be seen in this photograph is Sandon House, which was set back from the other properties. It would eventually de demolished and become the Lounge Cinema. Bridlington Library

The Royal Prince's Parade and Esplanade in the 1890s. One hundred years later, almost the entire Esplanade block would be amusement arcades.

Nick Laister Collection

harbours. The North Pier was completed in 1843 at a cost of £80,000. This was not a pleasure pier of the type that would be found in Blackpool or Brighton; it was a stone pier, the first part of a retaining wall to create a safe haven for Bridlington's large fishing fleet. It replaced the inadequate timber piers used for the docking of commercial boats, which had been rebuilt several times over the past few hundred years and needed constant repair due to their continuous battering by the sea. As soon as the North Pier was complete, work started on a new South Pier. By 1848, the two piers were complete, and the modern Bridlington Harbour was born. By 1866, when Bridlington was clearly becoming established as both major holiday destination and fishing port, the North Pier was extended.

But it was the opening of the Bridlington-Hull railway in 1846 that ushered in a new era for the Quay. Before that time, the main form of transport to the town was the stagecoach, which even from Yorkshire's industrial heartland would have taken longer than a day. From this time great expansion took place, and the Old Town would take a back seat while the Quay area blossomed into the famous Bridlington seaside resort.

As with many of Britain's great seaside resorts, the opening of the railway was the catalyst for investment in infrastructure and attractions. In Bridlington's case, this development was surprisingly rapid, because (unlike many seaside resorts of the time) public sector expenditure would outweigh private sector development in entertainment venues. This was accelerated in 1863 by the creation of the Local Government Board. But the ambitious plans to create a first-class seaside resort for the masses were not welcomed by all. Plans for a 'grand Sea Wall Parade', which would have been accompanied by improvements in drainage, were resisted by ratepayers. But the Board pressed ahead. The Sea Wall Parade opened in June 1867, and featured ornamental terraces, flower beds, shrubberies, grottos, seats and walks. In 1888, the Parade was extended and formally opened by Prince Albert Victor, the eldest son of Albert Edward, Prince of Wales (later King Edward VII), after which it was named 'Royal Prince's Parade'. One of the most notable buildings from this period was the Alexandra Hotel, built between 1863 and 1866, Bridlington's biggest and most lavish.

But what of entertainment venues for visitors? The town's amusements can be traced right back to the assembly rooms adjoining the Ship Inn (later the Britannia) on the south side of Prince Street. A range of entertainment was on offer, including dances and card parties (card parties were a common way to spend an evening during this period – a group would play card games around a small table whilst food and wine was served). Itinerant showmen, such as Robert Powell, 'fire eater, from London', were also attracted to the town.

The Victoria Rooms on the North Pier top were opened in 1848. The public rooms in this building included a ballroom, a reading room and a billiard room. This would be the town's primary amusement venue for almost 50 years, featuring such performers as Mr Colvil Dyke, conjurer and ventriloquist, and Miss Le Na, 'the Marvellous Clairvoyant'. The Victoria

Rooms were later used for cinematograph shows (from 1909, courtesy of the Corporation's own Bioscope machine) and, as we discover later, it would even house Bridlington town centre's first amusement arcade!

In 1876, Sheffield-based businessman JF Parker opened the Empress Roller Skating Rink on Beaconsfield Parade, but this was short-lived. A wooden Switchback Railway, an early forerunner of the roller coaster, was erected close to the sea north of Sands Lane in 1888, only

Royal Prince's Parade before the Floral Pavilion and Grand Pavilion were constructed. A far cry from the colourful fairground of today, this part of the seafront was the most exclusive part of the town, with toll booths clearly visible at the bottom of the photograph, designed to keep out the working classes. The Parade was certainly an elegant location in 1900, when this photograph was taken, as can be seen from the well-dressed ladies with parasols.
Nick Laister Collection

The Victoria Rooms pictured in c1900. In 1923, this building would become the first home of Premier Amusements, which still operates to this day in premises in Prince Street.
Bridlington Library

Gateway to the future: Bridlington's first amusement structure was the Switchback Railway of 1888 at Sands Lane. A forerunner of the modern roller coaster, it survived almost a quarter of a century before being demolished to make way for a residential development and amusement arcade.
Bridlington Library

An early view of the Switchback Railway. A large part of the Switchback site remained in amusement use until 1999, as the site of the Fun City arcade, built almost exactly on the site of the Switchback station.
Bridlington Library

three years after the country's first switchback opened in Skegness. This became a major attraction for the resort, creating an 'anchor' at the northern end of Bridlington's sea front, visible from the harbour. The Switchback became part of a collection of rides, including a helter skelter, in what was Bridlington's first amusement park. But land and property values prompted the ride's demolition in 1912, when a new residential development (Lamplugh Lane) was built on the site.

An early picture of the Switchback Railway in 1892, four years after its construction. Adjacent to the roller coaster was a set of swingboats. Bridlington Library

Esplanade at the turn of the 20th Century, looking towards the Harbour and Victoria Rooms. Within about 20 years, these private villas and lodging houses had converted their ground floors into shops. Only 20 years after that, they would all be changing again as the development of amusement arcades became seemingly unstoppable. Then, after another 20 years, the small front gardens that can clearly be seen on this photograph would disappear beneath ground floors extensions as permanent canopies were constructed right up to the pavement Nick Laister Collection

Above: A view of Royal Prince's Parade circa 1910, showing the Floral Pavilion and, behind, the wooden Grand Pavilion Theatre. The row of lodging houses behind the Floral Pavilion fronting onto Esplanade would gradually become amusement arcades, one of which would be Joyland. Nick Laister Collection.

Right: Looking up the Floral Staircase in 1924 towards the Esplanade. The building immediately facing the stairs would become Joyland in the 1930s. To the right is the Trocadero Café, owned by Rileys Dairies Ltd. Nick Laister Collection

The Victoria Rooms was to lose its dominance as Bridlington's only place of indoor enter-tainment, with a flurry of development activity in 'pleasure palaces' in the late 1800s/early 1900s. The People's Palace, a large concert hall and dance hall, was built on Quay Road in 1896 and would survive, albeit as a cinema and renamed the Hippodrome, until it was destroyed by German bombing in 1940. This was followed by the glass and iron Floral Pavilion on Royal Prince's Parade (1904), extensions to the Parade (1904-06) and the wooden Grand Pavilion (1906, demolished 1936). Cinematograph films were shown at the Grand Pavilion from 1906 by the Loyal Dominion Animated Picture Company.

NEW SPA - BRIDLINGTON.

The 1907 Spa buildings, pictured in 1911. The Spa was demolished in 1919 and a new Art Deco Spa Royal Hall was built to replace it. The Spa of today was built in 1932. Nick Laister Collection.

Richard Field & Son Ltd acquired Sandon House (located in the 'gap' that can be seen in the photograph on page 5) to open a café. Before construction of the mock Tudor building that currently stands on the site, Field's constructed a makeshift entrance on the frontage to advertise the café, which can be seen clearly in this photograph. At that time, the café was located inside Sandon House itself. This site would eventually become the entrance to the Lounge Cinema and, later, John Ling Amusements. The building to the left, in a much altered form, would later become Bay View Amusements. Bridlington Library

Princess Mary's visit to Bridlington on 7 September 1928. The Royal procession is pictured outside the Marlborough Café on the corner of Marlborough Terrace and Esplanade, and the Lounge Café can be seen to the right. The buildings between the Marlborough and Lounge cafes would become Bay View Amusements.
Bridlington Library

Away from Esplanade, development on the South Side also began in the late 1800s. The Spa Royal Hall remains the most prominent building on this part of the seafront, with the largest dance floor in the north of England and a delightful Edwardian theatre. However, the current Spa buildings were not the first on the site. The original buildings were developed in 1896, when the Whitaker Brothers of Horsforth, Leeds, purchased land lying south of the Harbour. The Spa was burnt down in 1906 and rebuilt in 1907 with an extended sea wall built between 1925 and 1928. The Spa was demolished between 1919 and 1925, following its acquisition by the Council, and a new Art Deco Spa Royal Hall was built to replace it, opening in 1926. Unfortunately, this burnt down in 1932 and was rebuilt that same year as it is today.

Ever since the growth of Bridlington as a resort in the 1880s, Yorkshire has dominated as the source of its visitors, particularly Hull, Leeds and Sheffield. Bridlington was often called 'Sheffield-on-Sea'. GW Travis, who had built Marlborough Terrace (in the same block as Joyland) and a number of other major Bridlington developments, heralded from that City, as did Empress-developer, JF Parker. And there would also be a strong Sheffield connection in the development of the town's amusement arcades including Joyland itself.

THREE

~

Early Amusement Arcades

"By the mid-1890s, shops devoted solely to 'automatic shows' were springing up in London. These early arcades were free to enter, but would often include additional entertainment in the form of freak shows or waxworks which customers would have to pay to see."

Barrons amusement arcade at Great Yarmouth was Britain's first seaside arcade, opening in 1897 in a temporary building. The replacement building, built in 1902, was designed by local architect AS Hewitt. This 2003 picture shows the arcade – still under the same family's ownership – one year before its closure. Nick Laister

Although it would grow into something much more than an amusement arcade over the years, Joyland – or 'Luna Park' as it was first called – started life as a simple slot machine arcade, and as such is a product of the huge growth in the use of amusement machines in Britain towards the end of the 19th Century.

Optical devices were believed to be the first form of slot machine. The camera obscura was one of the most successful early amusement machines, being a combination of education and entertainment. It showed a microscopic panorama of life outside the darkened booth, but it would not work on a dull day. An example of such a device certainly appeared on Brighton Chain Pier as early as 1824. This would eventually develop into the mutoscope, or 'what the butler saw' machine.

As with that other popular pastime, the cinema, the growth in the use of slot machines can be traced back to the activities of travelling showmen. The real boom in their growth was a product of the travelling fairground in the 1880s. Slot machines were rarely presented in arcades, but scattered amongst the other attractions of the fair. In this period, showpeople were also responsible for the growth of 'gaff shops', which grew up in the early 1900s, where travelling fairground operators would open in temporary indoor venues in the major cities over the winter months, often in empty shop units. By the mid-1890s, shops devoted solely to 'automatic shows' were springing up in London. These early arcades were free to enter, but would often include additional entertainment in the form of freak shows or waxworks which customers would have to pay to see. These early arcades, which by the early 1900s had started to appear in other big cities, were often drab affairs, spartanly decorated (although a small number were known to have been ornate), located in back street shops, often with no fronts, open to the elements.

Arcades at seaside resorts began to emerge almost in parallel. Small arcades could be found at resorts from the early 1890s, though most were small-scale temporary ventures. The Scarborough Promenade Pier Company registered its intention to provide machines for its customers as early as 1890. They were scattered around the pier, both outside pier buildings or along the main pier walkway. This was fairly typical of early pier attractions.

The first permanent seaside arcade was almost certainly opened in Great Yarmouth by a Mr George Barron. Barron was an amusement machine manufacturer who started out with an open-fronted automatic show in London in the

What a Married Man Ought to Know: Early amusement machines at Mablethorpe c.1932.

Arthur Plumb

late 1800s. The Barrons were also the first to provide cinematographic entertainment in London music halls. Barron formed the Inter-Changeable Automatic Machine Company and in 1895 he opened what is believed to be Britain's first permanently sited amusement arcade, in Islington, London.

But, as with the early travelling arcades and gaff shops, there was a showland connection to this amusement venture. Barron married into the Gray family of Norfolk showpeople and this resulted in him regularly visiting Great Yarmouth with his family's funfair and attractions. It was 1897 when Barron opened what is believed to be the first permanent land-based seaside amusement arcade on Great Yarmouth's sea front. Called the Jubilee Exhibition, its name celebrated Queen Victoria's Golden Jubilee, which was being celebrated that year. The temporary building contained a rifle range, electrical engraving (a machine that would engrave items, including coins), slot machines, mechanical models, fortune tellers, a fancy bazaar (market stalls selling seaside products) and an early type of moving picture show. The centrepiece was a steam-driven mechanical organ. The arcade also featured living exhibits such as The Harem and, most bizarrely of all, Beautiful Marie, the Giant School Girl, described as "a masterpiece of growing British humanity". To get the first season started, Barron exhibited a large stuffed whale and visitors paid a penny to view the curiosity. Passers-by were encouraged to enter by George Haughes, the Leamington Giant, standing at 7ft 4ins tall.

However, the Exhibition was short-lived. On 5th September 1901, a fire broke out in a barber shop next door and quickly spread to the adjoining Goode Brothers Academy of Dance and Sea View Hotel, before destroying the Jubilee Exhibition. This was a serious blow for the Barron family, as only one month earlier their insurance company had declined to insure the arcade due to the use of paraffin lamps in the back of the 'what the butler saw' machines.

Thankfully, due to the success of their other business ventures, Barron was able to reinvest. Soon he had built a permanent exhibition on the site and later the adjoining Sea View Hotel was purchased and a larger arcade, called the Paradium, was built, so named after the visitors who paraded along the seafront. Designed by local architect AS Hewitt, it opened in 1902 and became just as popular as the Jubilee Exhibition.

Machines in the early Barron arcade included a mechanical Fortune Teller, the Blacksmith (an early punch-ball) and a New Auto Piano (a forerunner of the jukebox).

The Barron arcade, which sadly closed in 2004, was run in recent years by George Barron's great, great grandson Stanley Barron.

Wheeler's Wonderland at New Brighton was another early seaside arcade and advertised itself in 1906 as having over 100 penny-in-slot machines. Early amusement parks also featured slot machines. Belle Vue in Manchester, often regarded as Britain's first amusement park, had an increasing number of amusement machines in the early 1900s. But in this period, permanent arcades were still rare, with most machines installed as supporting attractions in shops and public houses.

It wasn't until the late 1920s that permanent amusement arcades started to spring up at seaside resorts across Britain, including Weston-super-Mare and Plymouth. And, when our story returns to Bridlington, it will be seen that the town would soon be at the forefront of the development of the country's amusement industry in more ways than one.

Four

Amusement Arcades Come to Bridlington

"The first machine he left in a pub was delivered on a Friday. By the Sunday morning the landlord telephoned him angrily stating that the machine was out of order. On visiting the pub to look at the machine, he found that it was not out of order, just full of money!"

GEOFF GIBSON

In 1923, Premier Amusements was operating in the Victoria Rooms and was the first amusement arcade in Bridlington town centre. The entrance can clearly be seen behind the crowds, advertised (as were almost all amusement arcades of the period) as having 'Free Admission'.
Bridlington Library

Amusement arcades appeared in Bridlington very early in their development. Free-standing machines operated on the North Pier in Bridlington Harbour from the early 1900s, but the first arcade was Fun City at North Marine Drive, which was operated by a Mr Stephen Burgin. It is not known when it first opened, as it started out in a temporary building, but it was mentioned in Bridlington holiday guides from 1916 (despite the war).

By the 1920s, Bridlington was one of the top ten UK resorts (at number eight, ahead of Torquay, Skegness and Morecambe, according to the 1921 national census). With business booming, Fun City's temporary structure was replaced in 1923 with an art-deco building designed by Maurice Parkin. The arcade was built on the site of the earlier open-air amusement park, which had featured the Switchback Railway.

Amusements had found their way into Bridlington town centre by 1923. The main hall of the Victoria Rooms, until then used as a dance hall, became 'Premier Amusements'. The attractions in this early arcade included fairground-style sideshow games, a small selection of early wall-mounted coin-operated machines and stalls. Premier Amusements would move from the Victoria Rooms to Prince Street in 1933, when the Victoria Rooms were destroyed by fire.

Arabian Nights – Bay View Amusements opens

Bridlington's third arcade, Bay View, opened in 1930. It was owned by Charles William Pearson Gibson (known as William Gibson), and run with the help of his son, Raymond Gibson. The opening of Bay View is a significant development in the story of Joyland as it was the first arcade to open on Esplanade and would be Joyland's biggest competitor for many years.

Another view of Premier Amusements at Bridlington's Victoria Rooms.

Bridlington Library

Inside Premier Amusements in the Victoria Rooms.
Bridlington Library

A September 1927 photograph of Burgin's Fun City – Bridlington's first purpose-built amusement arcade – only four years after it opened. The arcade was built on the site of the Switchback Railway and remained open until 1999. Inside can be seen a range of sideshows: 'Madam Psycho A.B.I.M.S. – Palmist & Clairvoyant'; 'The Studio'; and 'The Whirling Tanks – Latest Game of Skill'. Bridlington Library

The Victoria Rooms on fire in 1933. Following the fire, Premier Amusements moved into a new unit on Prince Street, where it still operates to this day.
Bridlington Library

A magnificent photograph of the Royal Prince's Parade in the 1920s, showing the distinctive mock Tudor Esplanade Café and Restaurant, which would become the Lounge Cinema entrance and, later, John Ling's arcade. The building immediately to the left would become Bay View Amusements, the first amusement arcade on Esplanade.
Bridlington Library

William Gibson started in the slot machine industry as a manufacturer. His Hull estab-lishment was certainly not glamorous; he operated out of a small shed and hand-built machines, with the help of one of his uncles. His approach to delivering the machines was also far from glamorous. He would put them into his motorbike sidecar and drive them to local resorts, such as Hornsea and Bridlington, mainly for use in local pubs and would return on a regular basis to empty them. This business, despite being basic, was an immediate suc-cess, but it wasn't without its hiccups, as his grandson, Geoff Gibson, remembers:

"The first machine he left in a pub was delivered on a Friday. By the Sunday morning the landlord telephoned him angrily stating that the machine was out of order. On visiting the pub to look at the machine, he found that it was not out of order, just full of money!"

In the 1920s, William decided that he didn't just want to supply machines to pubs, he wanted to operate them as well. He was a very astute businessman. Witnessing the growth in the pop-ularity of seaside resorts, he saw the potential of filling a shop with slot machines. His first venture was in Skegness, where he opened a small amusement arcade. Typical of arcades of that period, there were not many machines, it was mainly filled with fairground-style stalls. He leased sections of the arcade to concessionaires, supplied the slot machines himself and allowed them to fill the rest of the arcade with stalls. Holiday camp king, Billy Butlin, who began his seaside career running hoopla stalls in the Lincolnshire resort, rented two stalls off him. Butlin left the Gibson arcade to start his amusement park venture, which eventually led to the creation of his holiday camp empire.

In 1930, William Gibson, along with his son Raymond and two daughters, Audrey and Muriel, opened Bay View Amusements. The shop unit, into which Bay View was opened, was small and built on the front garden of a house called Poplar Cottage, which was set back considerably from the Esplanade frontage. The large walled garden between the shop unit and Poplar Cottage (which was renamed Bay View Cottage) housed an orchard and provided Gibson with the potential to expand. He quickly got to work and extended the rear of the shop unit onto the site of the orchard, creating a long, narrow amusement arcade. The cottage at the rear then became the workshops.

Bay View had a good selection of early amusement games, but William Gibson knew that the property had more potential. There were several floors of accommodation above the arcade, so it was decided that they would take lodgers to supplement their income. One lodger was to become very famous.

TE Lawrence (better known as Lawrence of Arabia), seeking anonymity as Aircraftsman Shaw, spent the last few months of his RAF service with the Marine Craft Unit in Bridlington, in the winter of 1934-5. He supervised the winter overhaul and testing of ten fast armoured target boats stationed in the town. He had also stayed in Bridlington in service on other occasions between 1929 and 1933.

Three months after leaving Bridlington he was killed in a motorcycle accident. A sundial has been erected in the town to his memory.

The Joyland site

Although the first part of Joyland to open would be a small shop on Esplanade, the nucleus of the arcade would grow from the decaying carcass of a long-dead business which had been part of the Bridlington scene for many years.

The coaching and livery stables business that occupied a large proportion of the land onto which Joyland evolved, was operated by husband and wife, Matthew and Mary Knaggs. Mary, in particular, would become synonymous with the growth and success of the business. Born in Driffield in 1827, her father had originally bred donkeys and supplied them to Flamborough fishermen to convey freshly caught fish in pannier baskets from North Landing up to Flamborough village.

Fun City from the beach in July 1927.
Bridlington Library

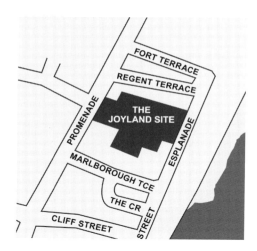

The street layout around the Joyland site. Joyland would eventually expand to cover a large part of this block between Promenade and Esplanade.

Nick Laister

Matthew and Mary married in March 1849, her arrival into her husband's family's coaching business almost coinciding with the arrival of the railway into Bridlington. The coming of the railways brought large numbers of visitors to the town and Knaggs would hire out carriages with guides to take visitors to North Landing and Flamborough Lighthouse. Tapping into this new tourist market, the business was expanding at just the same time as the development of Promenade, Marlborough Terrace, Esplanade and Regent Terrace was dramatically changing the appearance of this thriving area of the town.

Matthew Knaggs died in 1876, and was buried in Bridlington Priory churchyard. Following her husband's death, Mary continued to expand the Knaggs business interests in the town by opening a sweet shop at St John Street.

The buildings that made up the coaching station were very nondescript. There was a wooden shack, used as a booking office, at the front of the site in a large open forecourt. The house (named 'Talgarth') and stables were at the rear of the site.

Following Mary's death in 1899, the coaching business was taken over by her son, Arthur Knaggs. It was in the years after Arthur Knaggs took over the livery stables business that motor transport started. The livery stables were replaced with a garage for motor charabancs, the forerunner of today's luxury coaches, and Knaggs was the first operator in Bridlington to have motor charabancs, his first being called 'Majestic'. Built in London, Majestic was purchased in 1912 and became a tourist attraction in its own right. Many of Bridlington's visitors, who could not afford to ride Majestic, were content in just being able to see it and marvel at its technology.

Arthur Knaggs also had expansion in mind. Immediately adjacent to the coaching station was a small unit that had been occupied for many years by a artist and photographer called

View of Talgarth Livery Stables at the end of the 19th Century. The photograph shows a white horse and carriage ('London') about to enter the Stables. Note the shed with advertising sign attached. The building on the right is J W Shores photographer. The Stables and the site of Shores would eventually become part of Joyland.

Dora Wright/Charles Henson

The sale of horse-drawn vehicles at Talgarth Livery Stables, Promenade, Bridlington in c.1910. On the right is photographer JW Shores' premises. Adjacent to that is the small wooden office. At the rear of the site can be seen Talgarth House with a collection of stables, workshops and other outbuildings. The Forum's Promenade entrance building now stands on this site – Talgarth House is approximately on the site of Joyland's Dodgems and open yards. Dora Wright/Charles Henson

This charabanc is probably 'Majestic'. Purchased in 1912, it was commandeered in 1914 and went to the Strensall Army Depot near York. From there it was sent to France to help in the war effort. It is pictured in the front yard of the Knaggs coaching station. Behind is the house, Talgarth, which stood roughly in the centre of the current Joyland/Forum site. The entrance to the house is on the right, with the office entrance on the left. Dora Wright/Charles Henson

A view down the side alley, showing "A. Knaggs Order Office". A sign states "No Business on Sundays". By the time this photograph was taken (the early 1900s), the small hut in the previous photographs had been replaced by a (slightly) more permanent building.
Charlie Chinnery

271 - Bridlington - The Floral Staircase

The Floral Staircase on Royal Prince's Parade in c.1925. The row of buildings at the top of the Staircase is Esplanade. Riley's Trocadero café is to the left; the buildings on the right would eventually become Corrigan's amusement arcade. Nick Laister Collection.

John Waites Shores. Immediately following Shores' death in 1910, Arthur Knaggs acquired this unit to widen his frontage with Promenade.

By the 1920s, Arthur Knaggs had retired and the business was taken over by his son, Matthew Harrington Knaggs (born 1901, known as 'Mappy' Knaggs by his friends). During the First World War, he joined the RNAS as a driver and, although he helped out in the business after the war, his heart was not in it. Soon after taking over, things rapidly declined and Mappy decided to close it. From a pioneering stables to a motor garage, one of Bridlington's best remembered businesses of the 1800s and early 1900s had ceased trading and the site was left to rot for a number of years.

At the opposite end of the Joyland site, Esplanade in the 1920s was made up of a row of four-storey shops, lodging houses and private villas. The road was primarily developed in the 1820s and 1830s (including numbers 1 to 5, where the seeds of Joyland would be planted a hundred years later). By the late 1920s, most of the shop buildings along Esplanade had installed lightweight canopies, and it had become very busy with holidaymakers in the high season. This part of Bridlington was already showing potential to become the centre of activity for tourists, and for the few early entrepreneurs who realised this – such as William Gibson – the dividends would be huge.

One such entrepreneur was about to visit Bridlington. The arrival of a Mr Firth at a small retail unit on Esplanade was to change the face of Bridlington forever, and lead to the creation of the largest covered amusement complex in the country.

Busy view of Esplanade in the late 1920s before the arrival of amusements. The two units closest to the camera are Minnie Tipler's fancy goods and the Parade Motor Station. These would eventually become Joyland. The unit to the left of M H Tipler would become Luna Park.
Bridlington Library

FIVE

The Firth Family: Luna Park

"Arcades were still in their infancy, and to most of the town's visitors they were fascinating places, holding a great deal of mystique. Everybody wanted to see what was inside these mysterious Aladdin's caves."

Photograph looking north along Esplanade in the 1930s. The Corner Café can be seen to the left, and beyond that the canopies of Bay View and Luna Park. The glass building on the right is the Floral Pavilion. Nick Laister Collection

Engineering and Amusements

Luna Park, which was to become Joyland, had a very unspectacular start in a small unit on Esplanade that had formerly been a grocery shop. It was started by a man called Percy Firth. Firth was not travelling showman, nor had he any background in amusements, but he was a man of great foresight, who had identified the likely growth in amusements at the Yorkshire coastal resorts. Firth hailed from Brighouse in the West Riding of Yorkshire, where he ran a successful motor repair business. The move into amusements was a big gamble for a man who had been brought up in manufacturing (he was part of the famous Firth carpet family), although Firth was already a very successful man of not inconsiderable wealth.

When he arrived in Bridlington in 1932 and found the unit on Esplanade, he was not stepping into completely uncharted territory because he saw how successful Bay View, a few doors down Esplanade, had been over the previous couple of years. He was sure he could replicate that success. He knew how many people now flocked to Bridlington for their holidays; after all, he ran a major business in West Riding and knew that most of his staff went to Bridlington every summer.

He converted the shop into a small amusement arcade and set up a new company to run it, called British Amusements Ltd. Firth then acquired a number of slot machines to fill the arcade, but he decided that he wanted a unique major attraction as well, something that would differentiate it from the three other amusement arcades in the town. One of the big hits of the time was the Dodgems, which had been brought into the UK by a number of operators, including Lusse Brothers and Billy Butlin. Firth decided that such a ride could be a major attraction in Bridlington, and he was determined to build the town's first, despite his lack of space. The small Dodgem track was installed for the arcade's first season, in 1932, filling most of the arcade.

British Amusements Ltd was a real family-run operation. Although out of season there would rarely be a member of the Firth family in the arcade (Percy and his wife Olive were still based in Brighouse), at the height of the season, everyone helped out. His three daughters: Margaret, Connie, and Dorothy, all worked in the arcade in the school holidays. Percy even bought a property on Promenade where he and his family could stay.

Luna Park – Bridlington's Coney Island!

Firth's new arcade was an undoubted success. At the peak of the season it would be packed full of holidaymakers, often quite literally. The Dodgem track was very small, but it was hugely popular. Firth knew that his Dodgems would be even more popular if he could build a bigger track.

It was 1935 when Firth saw an opportunity for expansion. Another shop unit on Esplanade, in use as a café with apartments above, came on the market. It was a significantly larger unit than his current arcade and it came with a cottage and garden behind. Firth realised that this land could also be used for amusements, creating a much larger enterprise. This was a much bigger investment than his existing arcade, being a desirable sea front property on a frontage that was 'on the up'. So he drafted in his brother, James Walter Firth (1881–1963), to go into business with him and they jointly funded the acquisition of the property. The entire operation was moved into the new unit, which was then extended to the rear.

Firth took the opportunity to install a bigger dodgem track and to celebrate the move to this larger property, he named the arcade Luna Park, after the famous amusement park at Coney Island, New York. The new arcade was an immediate success, becoming one of Bridlington's most popular attractions.

The link between Esplanade and Promenade, which has been part of the secret of Joyland's enduring success, was achieved fairly quickly by Percy Firth, who realised that by acquiring properties he could provide a link between the seafront and town centre. This would act as a 'short cut' from the seafront to the shops, which he was certain would draw additional people into the site, as well as providing a prominent new entrance for the attraction. This would also create a very large tourist attraction – the biggest private operation in the town – with massive scope for introducing the latest rides and slot machines of the day. To create this large site would involve buying the partly derelict motor charabanc garage site behind, which had been operated by Mappy Knaggs.

Matthew Knaggs and the Luna Park Expansion

By the time of Luna Park's opening, Knaggs' garage had closed and lay derelict. Firth had been eyeing up the site for a couple of years, but unfortunately Mappy Knaggs did not agree with amusement arcades, and neither did his father, who still owned the site. At this period in Bridlington's history, many people frowned upon the arcades; they were still in their infancy and many feared the effects that such business would have on the town. Even as late as 1935, the proliferation of automatic machines was leading to serious local opposition. At a meeting at the Bridlington Literary and Debating Society, a Katheleen Dennett claimed that the Esplanade "has become a seaside branch of Hull Fair, full of cheap and tawdry merchandise". Others condemned "the encumbrance of North Pier with amusement machines". Mappy Knaggs was one such person; therefore he was not interested in selling his garage to Percy Firth if it was to become an extension of his Luna Park amusement arcade.

Percy Firth was a determined man, and was not going to let this minor hitch stop him. He hit upon an idea. As he owned Brighouse Motors, which repaired motor vehicles, if this company was seen to be buying the property, it would seem to Mappy Knaggs that the intention was to use the yard for its original use: transport. That way, he could obtain the property without Mappy Knaggs knowing that it would be for amusements. Of course, he could not allow his name to be linked to the deal. That is where his older brother, James, who was a co-owner of Luna Park but had no direct involvement in the business, could step in.

An appointment was made for James Firth to meet with Mappy Knaggs and view the property. He explained to Mappy who he was and where he was from, and produced all the necessary documentation to prove it. In March 1936, James Firth became the proud owner of the former Knaggs garage and wasted no time in knocking through the rear wall of Luna Park, creating an access directly into the garage area.

The newly acquired land behind Luna Park was large, and Percy knew that it would be impossible to develop it immediately. He decided that he would use some of the area to expand the amusements, and the remainder would be used on a temporary basis to provide something that was very poorly provided for in Bridlington: a car park. The cottage, office building and most of the stables were demolished.

To enable the arcade to be knocked through, Percy moved the Dodgems into the former Knaggs site. The area around the Dodgems was roofed over in the hope that when it rained, crowds would enter Luna Park and use its rides and attractions. The roof was an in-house job and done to a pretty low standard, but was only intended as a temporary measure. This 'temporary' measure would cause problems for many years.

In this expanded area, he also installed a Ghost Train in an area of open yard adjacent to the Dodgem track. This was not a small travelling Ghost Train, but was instead designed and built in-house and would remain in this location for 20 years.

One of the ride's features was a little cubby-hole, installed by the mechanics. If a couple of young women went in, members of Luna Park's staff would go into the cubby-hole and scare the life out of them. This was the forerunner of the modern day haunted walk-through with real life actors, but somewhat more informal, and the feature was only ever used when young women were on the ride!

Space for stalls and machines was made around the outside of the Ghost Train. Some of the existing buildings were made into a workshop and store rooms. The remainder of the former garage site was used as a car park. This entire site – the amusement arcade, fairground and car parks could be accessed directly from Promenade.

What Mappy's reaction was to this development of his family's garage is not known, but he must have been pretty annoyed that the 'wool had been pulled over his eyes' in that way. Nevertheless, putting aside Mappy's slightly damaged pride, he didn't come out of the deal too badly. He walked away with £10,000 from the sale of his yard, a lot of money in 1930s!

Joint ventures

In 1935, Bridlington's two big seafront amusement arcades had a hugely successful season. Arcades were still in their infancy, and to most of the town's visitors they were fascinating places, holding a great deal of mystique. Everybody wanted to see what was inside these mysterious Aladdin's caves.

The families running the two seafront arcades, the Gibsons (Bay View) and Firths (Luna Park), would become very close. William Gibson's son, Raymond, and two daughters, Muriel and Audrey, became friendly with the young Firths, particularly with Percy's youngest daughter, Dorothy.

William Gibson realised that the younger members of the families were becoming more involved and found an innovative use for them. He built a little cabin at the entrance to the Bay View arcade; when customers inserted six pence into the coin slot, a prize would appear, as if by magic. The younger members of the two families – Audrey Gibson and Dorothy Firth – used to sit inside this box and hand out the prizes. They would take it in turns to put the presents in boxes and drop them through a little hole. Of course, the customers were completely oblivious to the fact that this highly complex 'machine' was actually powered by two young girls!

The friendships blossomed quickly, and Dorothy soon became almost like a member of the Gibson family. She was a pretty girl, and had caught the eye of William Gibson's son, Raymond. Summer romance became a lifelong partnership, when Raymond Gibson married Dorothy Firth. After the marriage, Dorothy Firth left Luna Park and worked with her husband at Bay View. Eventually, they would have three children: Michael, Geoffrey and Angela, one of which would remain in the amusement business.

Six

Charlotte Yvonne Brown: The Birth of Joyland

"The bear escaped into the packed arcade; there was panic. Jack Hepworth always kept chloroform and a cloth in the back of the arcade, just in case this happened. He got the chloroform out, poured it onto the cloth, and put it over the bear. This put the bear out, so Jack and Raymond Gibson could drag it back to its cage."

GEOFF GIBSON

The Pleasureland fire, 6 May 1938. Charlie Chinnery

Sheffield Market to seaside empire

Percy Firth was not the only one to notice the growing popularity of the east coast seaside resorts and the fact that thousands of working people travelled by train every week to places like Scarborough, Bridlington, Withernsea and Skegness. And he was not the only one to want to take advantage of it. From her glove stall on Sheffield Market, Charlotte Brown could also see this very clearly and decided to expand her business interests into stalls and games serving resorts on the east coast. So successful would this venture become that Charlotte would soon have a major impact on the development of amusements in Bridlington.

Charlotte Brown was born in London in 1886. Little is known about her early life, but by the 1920s, she had moved to Sheffield and her glove stall was a regular fixture at the market. By the 1920s her stall was making enough money to enable her to hire staff to run it while she concentrated on matters elsewhere. During the summer months she would take lodgings at whatever resort she was operating from, while at other times of the year she would travel around fairs renting ground for her equipment as she went.

Establishing herself at Skegness, Charlotte found that stall games like darts, rings and 'roll-a-penny' were just as popular at the seaside as they were on the fairground and by 1927, with the help of her sons Sidney (Sid) and Harry, she was soon looking to expand to other east coast resorts.

Opportunity came knocking early. On a hoopla stall next to her at Skegness was a young West Country showman that Charlotte, Sid and Harry got to know very well. He had given up his run of fairs in the south west to bring his stall to the seaside where he was certain, like Charlotte, that he would make his fortune. This young showman was Billy Butlin.

Butlin spoke of ambitious plans to open a chain of amusement parks and had also been toying with the idea of opening holiday camps. He asked Charlotte to join him in this venture, as she had more experience and much-needed ready cash – but as she had her own plans, Charlotte refused. After all, he was a showman operating a hoopla stall and would need more than just enthusiasm to bring his dreams to life. With hindsight a golden opportunity had gone begging, but Charlotte wasn't to know that.

As the 1920s turned to the 1930s, Sid and Harry Brown started running stalls in other east coast locations, such as Withernsea and Cleethorpes and, by 1933, Charlotte was well established on the Quay at Scarborough harbour. The 19 June edition of the trade newspaper, World's Fair, reported from the resort on the Whitsuntide holidays:

> "On the Fish Quay under the very able banner of Councillor George Wilkie of Cleethorpes, a splendid park is now drawing record crowds. The set out of the ground is first class and the attractions are excellent and constitute the following: Councillor George Wilkie's gigantic mountain dipper or figure eight railway, also his auto skooter cars; the kiddies' Whip; stalls by Barnfield with his spider and fly game and his Bisley range; Charlotte Brown's pintables and other games; Albert Cox's box ball."

Renting of the former Knaggs yard

Despite her success, however, Charlotte's amusement business was still small and fragmented – and she still retained her stall at Sheffield Market. She was not happy at having her family split up in this way, so her aim became to bring everybody together in one place.

A chance meeting with a supplier of amusement devices at Sheffield Market was to prove a spark that would ignite Charlotte's aspirations. He offered to supply a number of coin-operated pintables in return for a share of the profits, on condition that she found somewhere to operate them. It was an offer Charlotte could not refuse and, with her established sites in Skegness, Cleethorpes, Withernsea and Scarborough, the obvious choice for her next venture was Bridlington. This new venture required a different type of location to the informal stalls she operated at other resorts – a permanent site was needed.

On arrival in the town it didn't take long before a suitable site was recommended to her. Permission for a cinema had recently been refused at this location because it was next door to a church and, consequently, the owner was looking for other opportunities. The site in question was the former Knaggs Yard, now owned by Percy Firth, and a deal was soon done enabling Charlotte to move in. The pintables were laid out in the open air; at night, she would cover them with tarpaulin.

It is easy to take pintables for granted now, but in 1935 they were the latest attraction and few visitors to Bridlington would have seen one. Unsurprisingly, they were a huge hit and with the success of this venture, and the proceeds from her family's other seaside stalls, Charlotte realised the next step was to open a permanent amusement arcade.

Little Joyland

Charlotte liked Bridlington. Of all the resorts she was operating in, she saw the greatest potential in the town. It had good rail links, an elegant sea front, good entertainment facilities, a beautiful harbour, and fantastic views of Flamborough Head. She decided that, not only was she going to acquire a permanent amusement arcade, the arcade was going to be in Bridlington. She was also fully aware of Percy Firth's success in his Esplanade shop unit, so she decided her arcade had to be on the Esplanade, where she could go into direct competition with Bay View and Luna Park.

She first leased a former shop adjacent to Luna Park. The building was a former sea front villa called Marshal House, which had been used as a fancy goods shop for a number of years, operated by a Miss Minnie Tipler. Charlotte opened her first permanent amusement arcade in time for the 1936 season, and she called it 'Joyland'. By the end of 1936, Luna Park and Joyland between them became two of Esplanade's most prominent attractions, and Brown and Firth developed a healthy competitive business relationship.

But for Charlotte this was not enough. Her ambition was to create Bridlington's biggest and most popular tourist attraction. The appetite of Bridlington's visitors for amusements was seemingly endless. In October 1937, she therefore took the next step with the acquisition of Marshal House from Minnie Tipler for the princely sum of £5,500.

Charlotte now had her sights set on Luna Park. Her small Joyland arcade was thriving, but she knew that Luna Park, with its direct connection through to Promenade, had the greatest potential for development as a large amusement complex. Whilst Percy Firth was taking advantage of the link, and operating his Dodgems and Ghost Train on the site, he was still using most of the available space as a car park.

Charlotte was a shrewd businesswoman and made it clear to Percy Firth that she wanted to buy him out. Unfortunately, Percy was still committed to continuing with the arcade, even though Charlotte was well aware that this was not his main business. Fortunately, his brother, James, was not quite so committed, as he was still much more involved with Brighouse

Motors, so Charlotte made him an offer he could not refuse. By the end of the 1937 season, she had acquired James's share of the business so was in partnership with Percy Firth in running Luna Park as well as her own Joyland arcade.

She was able to take advantage of this new arrangement by siting some of her stalls and games on the yard areas, which were not fully utilised, as she had two years before. But with only a 50% share of the Luna Park business, she was still not able to fully realise her ambitions. So, she continued her efforts to buy out Percy Firth's share.

Like most people at the end of the 1930s, Percy could see the international instability ahead, and his health had not been at its best. Most importantly, with the approach of the Second World War, demand for the services of Brighouse Motors was increasing. He therefore began to take more and more of a back seat in running the Luna Park business. By 1939, whilst still in partnership with Percy Firth, Charlotte was in reality running both Joyland and Luna Park alone.

Eventually, Percy Firth conceded and Charlotte bought out his interest in the Luna Park business, allowing her to merge the Luna Park site with her Joyland arcade. The entire site was renamed Joyland (of course, she wouldn't have dreamed of calling the entire site Luna Park!).

It could be argued that she was just in the right place at the right time, as in the late 1930s there was a major change in the way working class people spent their holiday. Whilst bank holidays had been in existence since 1871, it was the 1938 'Holidays with Pay Act', which entitled all industrial workers to at least one week's paid holiday a year, that caused a big explosion in seaside holidays. Seaside resorts like Bridlington, which were well placed to serve Britain's major industrial areas, experienced phenomenal growth in this period. Amusement arcade operators had never had it so good.

Whether by good timing or through her passion and persistence, by the outbreak of the Second World War, and in the space of just four years, Charlotte had progressed from owning a handful of pintables to presiding over the largest amusement arcade complex in Britain.

From Joyland to Pleasureland

It wasn't long after starting her Joyland arcade that Charlotte set her sights on further expansion. She knew that there was potential for Bridlington to have more amusement arcades, but she wanted to open one that would be different. All of the arcades were on, or very close to, the seafront; her idea was to open one in Bridlington's town centre, but ensure it was easily accessible from the seafront. She quickly found the ideal location. There was a small shopping arcade which provided a link between Prince Street and Cliff Street. What was special about this shopping arcade was that it created a link between two streets and Charlotte was convinced that this would be the key to the arcade's success.

Prince Street had been favoured as a place of residence by some of Bridlington's wealthier merchants and mariners, but by 1937 it was a thriving shopping street. On the site of what would become Pleasureland Amusements was the grandest house of all on Prince Street, home of the Rickaby family. The seven-bay, three storey house was built in c.1710 and was modelled on nearby Sewerby Hall. It was a big house for a big family, the Rickabys numbering 14, including staff. On the death of John Rickaby in 1860, the house started to be divided up into shops; by the end of the 1880s shop fronts had been inserted across the entire frontage.

The building was acquired by CG Southcott, a Hull-based tailor who had a chain of shops across the West Riding. In 1913, Southcott removed the tailor shop and replaced it with a shopping arcade, with small stalls on each side, linking Prince Street with Cliff Street. This became Shaw's Arcade in the 1920s.

Charlotte leased the shopping arcade in 1937 and it became Pleasureland, another instant success. The Brown amusement empire was expanding, but all was not exactly as it seemed. It was one of Charlotte's best-kept secrets that she did not actually own Pleasureland. The arcade was still under the ownership of the Southcott family. She had a very good reason for keeping it secret: the Southcotts refused to sell it and she knew that whilst every other arcade operator thought it was hers, it would be secure. She also knew that if other arcade owners found out that it wasn't hers, they would try and buy it from the Southcott family. It would be over 30 years, when her son Sid was on his death bed, before Pleasureland was finally bought by the Brown family.

On 6th May 1938, after Charlotte had been operating the arcade for a matter of months, the unthinkable happened. She had been out of town for the day and on returning to Bridlington, she was told that an amusement arcade in Bridlington was on fire. As there were very few amusement arcades in Bridlington at the time, her immediate thought was that it was one of her arcades. Driving to Promenade, she could see Joyland was still standing. She said to her driver: "Don't go down near Pleasureland, because it could be Pleasureland."

She was right, it was Pleasureland. It was a huge blaze that entirely destroyed the interior, with flames so hot that all the pennies in the machines melted together. Thankfully, the building survived, and reopened as Pleasureland again later in the season. Whilst the cause of the fire was never determined, Charlotte decided that she wanted a member of her family to oversee the place in future, to be her eyes and ears. She wanted to make sure that a disaster like this would not happen again. Harry took on this role on her behalf. The result of this decision was that Sid began to take more responsibility for Joyland. This division of responsibility was to form the basis of the arcade's operation for the next 30 years.

Bridlington's amusement heyday

In the run-up to the Second World War, Bridlington's other amusement arcades were also thriving. As competition grew, amusement caterers had to look for ever more weird and wonderful ideas to capture Bridlington's growing holiday trade. William Gibson, the owner of nearby Bay View Amusements, rented another shop unit on Esplanade and presented 'The Incredible Fasting Man', a man who was apparently abstaining from food for forty days and forty nights. For a penny, you could have the pleasure of seeing him sitting in what looked like a prison, with nothing more than a bed for him to lie on and a glass of water. However, as with many things in the amusement and side-show business, all was not what it seemed. William Gibson's grandson, Geoff Gibson explains:

> *"When midnight arrived, Bay View's arcade manager, Jack Hepworth, would creep down to the unit, taking with him a full meal for the 'fasting man'. The fasting man could also be seen wondering the streets in the early hours of the morning for exercise. But come six in the morning, he went back into his 'cell' and the door was locked!"*

One of Bay View's star attractions in the years leading up to the War was the zoo at the rear of the arcade. Admission was free; the idea was that it would draw customers through the arcade, and they would spend money as they went. Centre of attention in the zoo was a cage with two Himalayan mountain bears. Holidaymakers would crowd around this cage in fascination; it was something the likes of which had never been seen before in Bridlington. It was on one such busy day when the unbelievable happened: one of the bears escaped. Geoff Gibson takes up the story:

> *"The bear escaped into the packed arcade; there was panic. Jack Hepworth always kept chloroform and a cloth in the back of the arcade, just in case this happened. He got the chloroform out, poured it onto the cloth, and put it over the bear. This put the bear out, so Jack and Raymond Gibson could drag it back to its cage."*

Bay View zoo also featured about 20 monkeys and two chimpanzees. William Gibson also bred budgerigars, which he would give away as prizes in the arcade.

In 1938 came news that would shock Bridlington's amusement caterers. William Gibson, one of Bridlington's amusement arcade pioneers, died at the age of 49. Responsibility for the arcade passed to his wife, Annie Gibson, with the help of her son, Raymond, and her two daughters, Muriel and Audrey. However, it wasn't only Bridlington's amusement arcade community that were experiencing change at the end of the 1930s; war clouds were gathering over Bridlington's Esplanade.

Seven

Expansion and Investment

"A holiday visit was never complete without going on the machines in Joyland. My favourite was the Clutching Hand; we would return to our gas lit digs in North Street clutching two or three small souvenirs from this machine. I also remember the roundabout and the juke box at the end of the arcade."

RAY COCKERHAM

North Marine Drive in c.1945. H&E Baker's 'Sands Cottage Café' is in the foreground, and behind is Fun City, Bridlington's first amusement arcade. The industrial-style building behind the arcade's art deco frontage, which housed the slot machines, can be seen in this photograph. Nick Laister Collection.

With Joyland under her control, Charlotte Brown started making changes. The first thing she did was to close the car park, and expand the amusements across the entire site, from Esplanade to Promenade. Whilst Firth had introduced some amusement rides into this area, she wanted it all to be to a much higher standard; a permanent amusement complex. The Promenade end of the site thus became an open-air fairground. Charlotte erected a large fascia board sign, above an eight foot gateway, on the Promenade entrance, clearly advertising Joyland. The entrance was designed like the entrance to an amusement park – such as Manchester's Belle Vue or Blackpool's Pleasure Beach – where visitors were given the impression of leaving their everyday surroundings and entering another world.

The open-air fairground had a large range of traditional attractions: hooplas, darts, coconut shies, card games, and juvenile rides. The centrepiece was the two Swinging Gyms (also known as 'Swinging Cages'), an elaborate swing which would take riders over 360 degrees, whilst keeping them in a horizontal position. Local lad Dennis Tate, who would later become a mechanic at Joyland, remembers enjoying the fairground in the late 1930s, when Charlotte had first taken control of the site. His strongest memory is the Swinging Gyms:

> "I can remember what we called 'up 'n overs', like a big swing with a bar and a cage. You stood in the cage, counterbalanced, and you got yourself swinging right over. I remember using that and looking over the wooden fascia entrance down Promenade as I went over the top."

Charlotte quickly filled Joyland with the machines and games that she had been operating at seaside resorts around the country, and added newer electrically operated devices, such as electric pintables with flashing lights, buzzers and illuminated scores. One of the most notable types of machine in Joyland was the 'Allwin'. A ball bearing was shot by a sprung trigger towards a series of losing and winning cups via a spiralled track. These machines would dominate the complex for over 30 years. Other machines in the early Joyland were 1/2d and 1d pinball machines, fortune telling card machines, children's roundabout, rocking horses, motor cars, pick-up cranes and punch-balls.

The shop unit, in which Charlotte had first started Joyland, was now also connected to the main part of the site. Her staff always affectionately called the original section 'Little Joyland'. In the former yard area behind the old cottage, Charlotte opened the Joyland Zoo. This was a self-contained attraction, with an entrance fee.

In 1939, Charlotte made her biggest investment to date. She constructed a building at the Promenade end, to replace part of the open fairground with a covered arcade, and create a new entrance from the town. This still left an open yard in the middle where outdoor attractions could be located. Construction of the new entrance building was difficult, as Percy Firth had demolished the former garage buildings without removing all the services and original foundations. To construct a new permanent building on the site required more serious excavation. The garage also had a large petrol storage tank underground, which needed to be removed.

When complete, the building created an impressive entrance to the complex, through a large covered arcade. The exterior had art deco detailing, similar to cinemas of the period. Above the entrance were rooms that were intended to be used as flats. This building still stands today, although nobody has ever lived there; the counting house and offices were eventually installed there.

Charlotte erected a large sign over the entrance advertising the arcade. However, despite it being linked to Joyland on the Esplanade, she did not use the name Joyland. Instead, she

A Dodgem track attendant in the late 1930s. The light coloured uniforms were eventually phased out as they were found to be too hot to wear in the summer.

Walter Hoyes

called it 'Browns' Amusements'. One of the first attractions she introduced into the new building was the mirror maze, where, for a small fare, customers could lose themselves for a few minutes.

Sid and Harry Brown began to take more and more responsibility for the day-to-day management of the arcade. Sid and his wife, Margaret, settled in Bridlington very quickly; in fact, it wasn't long after they had made a permanent home in the town that Margaret became pregnant. In 1939, Sid and Margaret were the proud parents of a little boy, Peter, who would play a major role in the future development of Joyland.

Besides Sid and Harry, two other people had an important role in Joyland in the early years: George Laverick and Frank Ainley.

Ainley was the Manager of the complex, in charge of all the staff, and was also very involved in designing many of the building works as the complex expanded. He was a similar age to Charlotte, and met her when she was present-ing games in seaside resorts, being a traveller himself. He had remained loyal as she developed the business, becoming her 'right hand man'; Charlotte trusted him as much as her own family. He was a very well spoken man, who was polite with both customers and staff; indeed, many who knew him were surprised that such a seemingly well-educated man would work in the amusement trade.

When Joyland expanded through to Promenade, and Charlotte moved into the flat above the Esplanade entrance, so Frank Ainley moved in with her. As might be expected, this was always the subject of much gossip amongst Joyland staff! Ainley remained at Joyland as its Manager until his death in 1949.

George Laverick was Chief Mechanic, having spent his entire career either repairing machines or buildings. Laverick was 'inherited' from Percy Firth. He had already been involved in the Joyland premises before Charlotte took over, and had helped Percy Firth build up Luna Park. Laverick was something of a workaholic. As Chief Mechanic, he oversaw much of the development of Joyland before and during the War. Dennis Tate, who would later work for Laverick, remembers him:

"He had to work; it was his interest. He had a bad habit of going to broken electric cables, get-ting them and twisting them. And it would be live electric cables, just twisting them together, whilst they are live and machines are working. He was the same with the Dodgem track. Dodgem cables are on 110v DC, converted with a dynamo. He would do exactly the same thing with them; getting hold of them live and twisting wires together."

Percy Firth had already installed a Dodgem track in the centre of the site. Charlotte decided that this could be incorporated into a new larger covered area, centred on an enlarged Dodgem track; this new track would be the central attraction at Joyland for half a century.

Oh What a Lovely War

By 1939, just before the outbreak of the Second World War, there were seven arcades in Bridlington: Pleasureland, Palladium Amusements and Premier Amusements on Prince Street, Joyland on the Promenade and Esplanade, Bay View on Esplanade, Smith's on South Cliff Road and Fun City on North Marine Drive. It is no exaggeration to say that, in less than a decade, the arcades had dramatically changed Bridlington's sea front.

It is interesting to note that Bridlington's amusement arcade 'landscape' was largely mapped in that decade. The people who successfully positioned themselves at that time would go on to dominate the town's amusement industry for much of the rest of the 20th Century.

Sadly, planning for the future was the last thing on the minds of most people in 1939. Soon the War came along and the growth of Joyland along with the stability Charlotte had sought, was to be ripped apart. Only three years after she had pulled her family together in one place, Harry and Sid were called up.

The impact of the War on Bridlington was severe, with the resort reportedly empty of tourists during high season. The town also suffered serious bombing, so it is not surprising that it was not a preferred holiday destination. However, the impact of the War on Joyland was largely positive and the business prospered throughout the War years.

The blackout placed severe restrictions on the operation of the arcade. To get over this problem, the Esplanade end of Joyland was closed, and all customers had to enter via the new Promenade building. Customers entered through a door and down a small passage, formed concertina-like so that the light didn't shine out onto the street. The Dodgems, a snack bar, and a number of machines (all at the Promenade end) were operational throughout. The penny slot machines were kept running by the skeleton staff. The crane machines, however, eventually fell out of use as there were no prizes to put in them.

Although only part of Joyland was in operation, and Bridlington was suffering from a lack of visitors, the arcade remained reasonably busy. Joyland was ideally suited to forces personnel with money to spend during brief leave periods. There were a lot of soldiers billeted and

Harry Brown pictured in Pleasureland in 1939 with Sid Brown's baby son, Peter.

Peter and Linda Brown

In 1933, following a major fire which destroyed the Victoria Rooms, Premier Amusements moved into the Princes Hall on Prince Street. This photograph shows the arcade's impressive frontage in the 1960s. Note that they still advertised free admission, and 'Bingo' was prominently promoted. Anthony Shaw – Premier Amusements

training in the area, many staying in empty houses in the town, and spending freely in the amusement arcades. Joyland even had some soldiers billeted upstairs in the stock room. The amusements thrived on this and Joyland became a major local meeting place.

Local boy Terry Waddington remembers how popular the complex was with Polish troops billeted in the town:

"Joyland had a bumper car arena, so we would wait until a soldier boarded a car alone, then run across and ask if we could ride with them. We were rarely refused, though the management were not too happy about it and were always throwing us out."

It was this combination of high spending military personnel and minimal staff costs that the resulted in the arcade's wartime success. Charlotte was already beginning to reap the rewards of her astute business decisions and hard work.

Sidney Brown with his son, Peter, in the 1940s.

Peter and Linda Brown

Bay View in the War

Bay View, Bridlington's other major amusement arcade on Esplanade, also continued to operate throughout the War. And, like Joyland, it was left in the very capable hands of the women. Like the Brown brothers, Raymond Gibson was called up. He did five years in the Merchant Navy, going on convoys to America. The arcade was operated during this period by his wife, Dorothy, his mother and his two sisters, Audrey and Muriel. Whilst the War was a busy time for Joyland, as Bridlington's central attraction, it was somewhat quieter for Bay View as it only had an entrance on the seafront, which was much quieter than the town centre. The arcade was only open at weekends outside the main season, but it was boosted by being located next door to the soldiers' canteen. Audrey Black, Raymond Gibson's sister, remembers:

"During the War the soldiers and air men used to come in. Mother and I had to run the arcade just to try and keep the expenses going. We used to open when we wanted, and shut when we wanted! It was just to try and keep money coming in. A little bit to help out."

Right: Olive Firth pictured after the Firths had sold Joyland, in 1953, the year of Percy Firth's death. Alongside her is her second husband Jim Booth.

Geoff Gibson

After the War

After the War, stability returned to Joyland and the rest of the town's amusement arcades. Sid and Harry Brown returned, and were able to get straight back into the running of the arcade. If anything, they were more involved than ever before. With the arcade's success through the War years, Charlotte was able to invest considerably in its development. She improved the buildings and introduced new games and machines. A new children's roundabout was also installed adjacent to the Esplanade entrance, along with a new ice cream kiosk.

One of the main new attractions in this period was the Winchester Rifle Range, a large shooting gallery, using real ammunition.

The immediate post-War years also brought further happiness to the arcade, with another little addition to the family. Sidney and Margaret were the proud parents of a little boy in 1946, who they called Robert. Robert and Peter, who by now was eight years old, lived in the flat above the Esplanade entrance with their parents and grandmother.

By the late 1940s, having finally acquired the last few remnants of the Joyland properties that she hadn't managed to secure prior to the War, Charlotte was in her element guiding Joyland's growth and expansion. Most of her gambles seemed to pay off and her approach was undoubtedly influenced by her other main interest: horse racing. She was a regular at the races, and often gambled significant sums of money. She also owned horses and greyhounds, an interest that her sons would continue. She had a dislike and distrust of banks, keeping most of her takings 'upstairs' in the flats above the Esplanade entrance to the complex.

As the years passed, Charlotte slipped further into the background, controlling her business operations almost entirely behind the scenes. By the end of the 1940s, she rarely dealt directly with her staff. If she wasn't at the races, she would usually be found in her flat above Joyland's Esplanade entrance. Here, her senior staff would regularly report back to her. That was how she liked to run her business. Most of the other staff rarely saw her, and never spoke to her.

Sid and Margaret pictured in 1947 with Peter and new baby Robert.

Peter and Linda Brown

The Death of George Laverick

In the immediate post-war years there was a row of storerooms next to the Winchester Range. A shocking discovery was made here early in 1950. George Laverick was well past retirement age but still in charge of the mechanics at Joyland and still part of Charlotte's close circle of senior staff. Mechanic Dennis Tate takes up the story:

> "He had gone into the Workshop, into one of the store rooms. Somebody said: 'Where's George? I haven't seen him for an hour.' Then we just walked in and he was laid out dead."

Of course, everyone immediately thought that he had died of electric shock, but it was simply heart failure.

Laverick's replacement was Walter Hoyes. He had started at Joyland in May 1950 as a maintenance engineer. A trained turner, Hoyes had already caught Charlotte's eye. She had realised that slot machine technology was advancing at such a pace that they couldn't just take on a school leaver and hope that he could 'learn on the job'. They needed someone with real training, real knowledge, and Hoyes fitted the bill

Before the season started, Hoyes was thrown in at the deep end; he was asked to repair Joyland's biggest ride, the Dodgems. The Dodgem cars had become increasingly unreliable and had deteriorated into an appalling state over the years, so much so that the mechanics could not get the ride working. This would be the perfect way for Charlotte to find out whether Hoyes was the right choice for this senior post; he would either sink or swim. Thankfully, Hoyes succeeded in getting the Dodgems into a reasonable condition before the season started, and as the season progressed, his expert work on the ride resulted in it being fully restored.

The next few years became very interesting for Hoyes, as he became more acquainted with the arcade, its equipment and – most importantly – its shortcomings. The arcade had to be entirely rewired to conform with new Electricity Regulations. This was a big job, but it was completed in good time, with new lighting throughout the arcade. The powerhouse, from where the arcade's electricity was generated, had a complete refit under Hoyes' direction.

Hoyes spent many long hours in the Joyland workshop, making parts for machines. Besides his lathe, he had a huge cupboard with all the screws and other important equipment, everything being carefully filed and labelled. Robert Brown remembers:

> *"We used to go into his workshop and we would say, 'Half a dozen number tens, please, Wally.' And it was like going into an ironmonger's shop. He'd open this cupboard, and there were all the screws in boxes. You see, it was all nuts and bolts, screws and wood."*

Into the 1950s

In the 1950s, Joyland continued to thrive. As with many other seaside arcades and amusement parks in this period, it enjoyed its longest and most stable period of popularity. It seemed that – no matter what – the arcade was packed. At times it was so busy you quite literally could not move inside – as one mechanic said: "it was so busy that you could almost walk across peoples' heads"!

Among the amusement machines all around Joyland were side stalls, similar to those you would find at a travelling fair: darts, laughing clowns and rifle ranges being examples. There were several snack bars, one at either side of the Promenade entrance, and one adjacent to the Esplanade entrance. There was also a little children's roundabout.

At the heart of all this, there was still the huge Dodgem track in the middle of the complex. Regular holidaymaker, Chris Youhill, remembers spending many hours on the Dodgems in the late 1940s:

> *"The Dodgems were the finest in the world (to me at any rate) – there were 20 cars – four each in five different colour schemes. I was so addicted that I knew them all like old friends – and around Easter, after the Winter closure, you were allowed to stay on free all one particular day in order to clear the winter off the track and the overhead mesh."*

There were wooden signs at each corner of the Dodgems saying 'sixpence'. But these would be

Margaret Brown standing outside the Esplanade entrance to Joyland in the 1950s. Behind her is the Bingo, with a fine display of prizes. A coin-operated weighing machine is to her right.
Robert Brown

This photograph was taken during the winter maintenance period in the early 1950s. In the background is the Promenade end of the arcade, the roof of which was felt-covered and was being replaced and re-tarred by some of the staff in the photo. The roof was demolished in the early 1960s and was replaced by a modern one. The staff in the photograph were having their morning tea break. Pictured: (back row) Jeff Hobgard, Albert Templeton, Fred Shields, Joe Brown, Dennis Tate, (front row) Walter Hoyes, Stan Walker, Cyril Crane, Joe Lowery.
Dennis Tate

The staff at the Joyland Snack Bar in 1949. The manageress of the snack bar, Mrs Ninette Potts, is third from the left. The snack bar was located at the Promenade end of the complex. Mrs Potts also cleaned for Mrs Brown in her flat over the Esplanade entrance. Kenneth Potts

changed, depending on how busy the arcade was. When Sid wanted the price to be changed he would go to the end of the Dodgem track and wave his hand. One of the men had to go and lift the wooden sign out of its holder, turn it round, and it would then say 'shilling'.

During this period, Joyland still featured animals, although the pre-War zoo had closed. Monkey cages were installed behind the Dodgems; there was no charge to view them, the theory being that it would draw people to the centre of the arcade.

Sid had the place running like an efficient machine. Throughout the day, the arcade would be constantly patrolled by his mechanics. A closed attraction meant lost money, so when there was a breakdown they moved straight in to solve the problem.

Sid always stood at the Centre of the arcade by the cash box. He rarely sat down and, standing at this point, he could see most of the arcade. He was not only watching the customers; he was also watching the staff. He knew that many of them were stealing, and to an extent, he accepted that because, as he said on many occasions, "we have to make money for them to steal money". But he still needed to ensure that he wasn't being ripped off, particularly by the temporary seasonal employees.

It was also well known amongst staff that Sid could lip-read. They all learnt this eventually, sometimes the hard way. Mechanic Dennis Tate recalls Sid's ability:

"I was a keen swimmer. He came around to me one day, at a time when we used to finish our shift at eleven o'clock at night. I used to go swimming then. I started talking to some of the lads. 'Are you coming swimming with me tonight?' 'Oh, yes, we're going', they said. So Sid came up to me and he said, 'If any of them are asleep in the morning, you are in trouble.' He had seen my lips move!

"Next morning he came round and said, 'Dennis, can you get the rest of the lads to go swimming with you?' 'Why?' I asked. 'Your lads are the only ones that are awake!'"

In 1952, another family member was to join the team: Charlotte's nephew, Jack Henry. Jack played a major role in the running of Joyland and effectively acted as General Manager of the complex, a replacement for Frank Ainley. When Sid was away, Jack would take overall charge. This sometimes caused resentment amongst more senior staff who were not family, as Dennis Tate explains:

Sid Brown in the 1950s.

Peter and Linda Brown

Right: Sid Brown pictured outside Joyland with his son Robert. Behind can be seen a cabinet of 'Allwin' machines. The small elephant that can be seen in the machine on the left would give a prize for 6^D.

Robert Brown

"*Jack Henry liked to show his authority. I remember on one occasion, Sid turned around to me and said, 'Den, I'm having to go away for a couple of days. I want you to stand there where I stand and keep an eye on things.' I was the tallest of the mechanics, so that made sense. Like Sid, I could see over what was going on. 'Just keep an eye on things like I do.' So, I stood there for the day. Eventually, Jack Henry approached me and said: 'What do you think you are standing around here for? You should be out there working.' I said, 'Sid told me I had to stand here while he was away for the two days.' 'It doesn't matter what he said. I am in charge,' said Jack. I said, 'Sid's my boss.' He said, 'That doesn't matter, I'm telling you to move now.' So, when Sid comes back I said, 'I'm sorry, Mr Brown. I couldn't stand there because Jack told me I had to move.' Sid then said: 'When I am not here, Jack is in charge.'*"

For Joyland staff, hours were long and the rewards were low. Former mechanic, Ron Stockwell, who worked at the arcade in the late 1940s, remembers:

"*We used to start at ten in the morning, sometimes nine, and then finish at about ten or eleven at night. Seven days a week. It could be three o'clock in the morning when we finished on the day we emptied the machines. The men were given only two ten-minute breaks – one at lunchtime, and another in the evening – to allow them to go out and get their tea.*"

Joyland stalwart Jack Henry, pictured with Sid Brown's son, Peter.

Peter and Linda Brown

Counting money was the main task at the end of every week. In the beginning there was no counting machine and the coins were all hand-counted or weighed. There was a room upstairs over the Promenade entrance which was called the 'Copper Room'. All the pennies were carried up to this room, counted, placed in five-pound bags and sent down a chute. This was usually Jack Henry's job. In this room there was a large weighing machine, that in a former life was probably used to weigh potatoes. The coins were placed in a large brass scoop using a lead weight as a balance. The lead weight was made up to be specifically five pounds worth of pennies. Similar scales were used in Pleasureland.

There was a further counting room in Charlotte's flat above the Esplanade entrance. This one was for other coins, pound notes and silver.

Every Wednesday morning, the money was wheeled down the street on a flat barrow

Left: Ron Stockwell with his cycle. Ron was a mechanic at Joyland during the 1960s. To the right of Ron is a Joyland 'change man' whose name is not known.

Ron Stockwell

Happy families: Sid and Margaret Brown with their sons, Peter and Robert, in Joyland. Behind can be seen a 'working model' machine called 'The Watchman'.

Robert Brown

to the bank at the corner of Queen Street. This was an operation of almost military precision, but with meagre security precautions. Two mechanics would pull the cash mountain down the street, covered in a tarpaulin. One of the Browns would walk on ahead. This is a tradition that amazingly continued into the 1970s, after which the money was then transferred in the boot of a car!

And so it went, week in, week out. Mechanic Dennis Tate remembers the tricks he used to play on customers to make the day pass more quickly:

"A person wanted six pence, so he would give you six pence. You would pick up seven coins. You would hand three coins out to the customer, then you would find three more coins, and slide the seventh back into your hand. Now that customer would look, and he would see that coin slide back [into your hand]. And they counted: one, two, three, four, five, six. 'You're trying to rob, aren't you?' 'What do you mean, Sir?' 'I gave you sixpence.' 'And you wanted six pennies, didn't you?' 'Yes.' 'What have you got in your hand, Sir?' 'Six pennies, but I saw you slide that other one back.' I said, 'It isn't seven pennies for sixpence, Sir. It is six pennies for sixpence. If I give you that other penny, I am going to be out of pocket.' Time and time again, they would stand there counting. We used to do it just for fun, to break up the season."

Dennis also remembers that children had tricks that were much worse than his own:

"We used to get these kids coming in using knives under the cash box to try and scrape pennies out. They were wood fronted draws, and in summer the wood used to contract and you used to get a little gap which was as thick as a penny. The kids used to come up with a knife trying to pull the pennies out."

Season's End

Being a seasonal operation (Easter to September), most of the staff were laid off at the end of each summer, although key people would be kept on all year round to maintain and repair the buildings and machinery.

The few who were retained on a permanent basis had a fixed set of tasks for the closed season. The first job was to move all the machines in the open yard under cover. The staff were then given a month's holiday. Then they would start maintenance work in earnest; painting, building, woodwork, machine stripping and other repairs. This work continued until Easter week.

Throughout this period, the 1930s-built Ghost Train was still operating in the open yard. Although still fairly popular, it was becoming old and was certainly not taking the riders it once did. By the winter of 1951–1952, it was decided to replace the ageing structure with an

'Ark' ride (a large, fast roundabout), built by Burton-on-Trent ride builders Orton & Spooner. The Ark, which was named the 'Chariot Racer', was acquired from Corrigans, a prominent Yorkshire fairground family who had recently opened an amusement arcade in the same block as Joyland. Young Peter Brown had the task of joining his father, Sid, to view this new ride, which was stored above Corrigan's Scarborough arcade.

The Chariot Racer opened for the 1952 season and was a reasonable success. However, by the end of the 1953 season, Charlotte decided to advertise it in trade paper the World's Fair. The advert appeared in the 5 September 1953 edition, stating:

> *"For sale, Chariot Racer, 24 Horses, 6 Chariots, Orton and Spooner make, A real good flash, In very good condition. Can be seen working until the end of September at Brown's Amusements, Joyland, Bridlington."*

No buyer was found, and the Chariot Racer would remain a central feature of Joyland for the next two decades.

Success

Like Joyland, Harry Brown's Pleasureland enjoyed massive success in the 1950s. Ted Cooper, a writer in trade paper World's Fair, wrote about the arcade in August 1956:

> *"Pleasureland, with entrances in Prince Street and Cliff Street, is a smart place, both internally and externally, with gay neon signs to attract the public. The internal lighting is particularly pleasing, especially when one looks along the entire length of the arcade."*

Joyland engineers pictured in the open yard during the construction of the Chariot Racer ride in 1952. Pictured: (top row) Walter Hoyes, Joe Brown, Fred Shields, (middle row) Dennis Tate, Joe Lowery, (front row) unknown, Stan Walker, Cyril Crane, Sid Smith. Dennis Tate

In addition to the large array of slot machines, other attractions in the arcade at the time included Bingo, a Skee Roll, a Bisley shooter, an air gun trainer and all the latest slot machines.

In the same report, Cooper also wrote affectionately about Joyland:

"…Their chief premises are at Joyland, the largest amusement centre in Bridlington. With striking frontages on to the Parade and Promenade, Brown's is a landmark in the town. The external colours are cream and pale green, with red and green neon lighting and the Promenade entrance is flanked by cafes and snack bars. The adult rides are the Dodgems – with a well-painted 'grotto' setting – and the Chariot Racer, a machine with smart extended front and a general look of newness about it that does credit to its owners. At either entrance is

Pleasureland in the 1940s.

Dennis Tate

A delightful late 1950s view of Esplanade out of season. Joyland can clearly be seen to the right, shutters down, with maintenance work being undertaken on the sign. To the left of Joyland is The Lounge (cinema and café), with Bay View Amusements beyond.

Bridlington Library

located a modern juvenile to ride, and a selection of the latest coin-operated rides offer a wide choice for the children. The games and side attractions are well laid out and the uniform and nicely lettered fascias add to the general smartness of the park."

The power Charlotte had over her sons was best illustrated by the events of a rainy day at Pleasureland in the early 1950s. It was pouring with rain, and the wind was blowing through the arcade. Although Pleasureland now has glass doors, and is protected from the elements, in the 1950s there were only posts and shutters, so when the arcade was open to the public, it was open to the wind and rain as well. On this particular occasion, the wind was blowing the swag (the colloquial name for prizes that can be won in amusement arcades and fairgrounds) off the counters. Harry was not at the arcade at that time, so Manager Dennis Tate decided to close the shutters to try and stop the wind blowing through. It worked, and the staff could stop fighting against the wind, and start dealing with the customers.

On Harry's return, however, he was not happy to see the arcade partially closed, because he knew that his mother would not like it. He stormed in and shouted: "My mother doesn't want this place closing down at this time in the evening. It has to stay open!"

By the late 1950s, Charlotte had expanded her seaside operations beyond Joyland and Pleasureland. She had installed a large new ride on the South Promenade by the Spa complex, called 'Brown's Electric Super Cars'. Reporting on the ride for World's Fair newspaper in August 1956, writer Ted Cooper described it as: "…a lovely ride laid out around colourful flower beds and rockeries…" The site of Brown's Electric Super Cars is now a small, council-owned children's amusement park called 'Kiddies Corner'.

Meanwhile, Back at Bay View Amusements

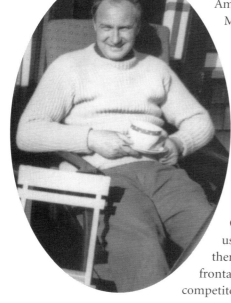

After the War, Bay View was still Joyland's biggest competitor. The arcade had remained open throughout the War, but when it ended, there was still much work to be done to rebuild it to the leading attraction it once was.

When Raymond Gibson returned from the war he became the driving force behind Bay View. His sister, Audrey, had married and left the arcade, and his mother had died. But Raymond was looking to the future and, just like Charlotte Brown at Joyland, he was working hard to expand his empire. His first step was to acquire Smith's Amusements on South Cliff Road, which he opened as South Cliff Amusements. By this time, Raymond also had two sons and a daughter: Michael, Geoffrey and Angela.

In the 1950s, there were three amusement arcades on Esplanade. Joyland and Bay View had been joined by Jolly Spot, which was located next door to the latter arcade. It could be said that Bay View missed a trick here, as Gibson had let an opportunity to consolidate his existing arcade slip and allowed a newcomer onto a seafront which Bay View and Joyland had previously dominated. The 'newcomer' was Edwin Corrigan of the well-known Corrigan fairground family, who had decided to make a permanent base at Bridlington and bought one of the Esplanade shop units.

Realising that he had allowed a newcomer onto his patch, Raymond Gibson made every effort to acquire the Jolly Spot from Corrigans. By the late 1950s, Raymond eventually bought Jolly Spot and used it to extend his arcade. Whilst Jolly Spot was only a small arcade and therefore did not increase Bay View's floorspace significantly, it made the frontage a lot bigger, virtually doubling its size, and making it a more serious competitor to its larger neighbour.

The Wonderland Gardens at Bridlington pictured in the late 1950s, with the Grand Pavilion Theatre (1937) to the right. These gardens are now the site of Leisure World swimming pool. Behind the gardens can be seen Esplanade, with 'Shaw's – The Holiday Shop' clearly visible. In the 1960s, Shaw's would become Corrigan's amusement arcade. Nick Laister Collection.

Bay View in the 1950s, with its expanded frontage. Standing in the centre of the photograph is Jack Hepworth, who worked at Bay View for 40 years. His stay at Bay View was only interrupted by a one year stint at Joyland. Behind can clearly be seen the Lounge Cinema. Geoff Gibson

Jolly's Café and Marlborough Café and Restaurant on the corner of Marlborough Terrace and Esplanade. Jolly's served "luncheons, teas, suppers, ices". Other cafés on Esplanade in the first decades of the 20th Century were Field's Oriental Café and Riley's Trocadero.

Bridlington Library

Having acquired South Cliff Amusements and Jolly Spot, Raymond Gibson was on a roll. He got wind that the nearby Corner Café (on the corner of Esplanade and Marlborough Terrace, a building that had been used as an officers' mess during the war) had been put on the market. Within five minutes, he was in the Corner Café and had secured the deal. He never operated amusements in the Corner Café, but instead rented it out to tenants, who used it for catering and as a public house. The building eventually became Gray's Inn (now the Hook and Parrott) and became a place where amusement caterers would congregate after a day's work.

Wes Walker, son of leading Bridlington amusement caterer Brian Walker (Harbour Top Amusements, Casino Royale), remembers the pub from the days when you could barely get served:

"The bar, its atmosphere and conglomeration of characters that shall never be replaced from which generated a million funny stories, would put shame to the entire comedy writing fraternity. Ex-RAF George Gray used to marshal the place. Silvio Rossi, the lovely cherubic gentleman who ran Notarianni's next to the Harbour Top Amusements on Prince Street for nigh on fifty years, was a regular. He was as much a part of the strong show fraternity, in my opinion, as any showman. A truly lovely, generous character who weathered being interned during the War to make Notarianni's an exceptional business."

By the 1950s, Bay View and Joyland had similar frontages onto Esplanade, both approximately the same size. In fact, people often mistook Bay View for Joyland, and expected to be able walk right through. Raymond Gibson's son, Geoff, remembers:

"We used to get a lot of people on Saturday morning walking through Bay View with their suitcases. They kept getting the two arcades mixed up. They thought Bay View was Joyland, and were using it as a short cut. We used to say to ourselves, 'Don't say anything to them!' They would get to the bottom and have to walk all the way back again."

Elsewhere in the town, Fun City on North Marine Drive – Bridlington's first amusement arcade – was acquired by amusement caterer Chris Thompson in 1953, who gradually refurbished and upgraded the original building. Following Chris Thompson's death, the arcade was taken over by his son, Manny, and his wife, Margaret.

A passer-by looks into the magical world of Bay View in 1954. To the right of the entrance is the 'Treasure Cave' novelty machine which gives "A Prize Every Time". Inside the arcade can be seen the Bingo, as popular in the 1960s as it is now.

Geoff Gibson

The 'Toys & Novelties' kiosk at Bay View in the 1950s with a children's coin operated ride adjacent. Inside the arcade can be seen Bay View's rifle range.

Geoff Gibson

The Death of Charlotte Brown

After running Joyland for over 20 years, Charlotte Brown died on 17 December 1957, aged 71. Her obituary appeared in showmen's trade paper World's Fair on 28th December 1957:

"Mrs Charlotte Brown, an amusement caterer in Bridlington for many years and one of the largest ratepayers in the town, has died in a Harrogate nursing home at the age of 71. She went to Harrogate for the Spa treatment three weeks ago, collapsed and since that time has been in a nursing home. In addition to her business interests in which her sons Harry and Sid assisted her, Charlotte Brown was a racehorse and greyhound owner. One of her latest racehorse

acquisitions was the steeplechaser Prudent Star. She was also the owner of several greyhounds which raced at Craven Park in Hull."

Her funeral service was held at Christ Church on 20 December 1957.

Charlotte's was a classic rags to riches story. She had seemingly overcome all obstacles and turned her dream of creating an amusement empire into reality. In doing so, she had changed the face of the Bridlington seafront forever, a legacy that still lives on to this day.

Charlotte was gone, but the story of Joyland was far from over. Her two sons were well-groomed and ready to take Joyland forward into the 1960s.

By the 1950s, Burgin's Fun City had become Thompson's Fun City. Built in 1923, this was Bridlington's first purpose-built amusement arcade.

Pete Tei

Joyland's Esplanade frontage pictured in the late 1950s.

Pete Tei

EIGHT

Harry and Sidney Brown: Stability and Success

"It was fun to explore, as it rambled back from the main entrance on the seafront through a maze of buildings to the back entrance. In the middle were a couple of rides in an area with a glazed roof. I can remember a little juvenile platform ride and an Ark…it seemed a fast ride to a little kid.

"The two things I remember most clearly were the smell (which was a glorious mixture of disinfectant, hot dogs, candyfloss and electric arcing) and the old mechanical slot machines which were almost museum pieces, even then. Whereas the other arcades in the resort seemed bright and modern, Joyland was dark and mysterious."

JOHN WARDLEY

The 'Super Electronic Skee-Roll' machines were a major feature of Joyland in the Sid and Harry years.
Reg Spencer

To the outside world, there was little noticeable change in Joyland's appearance or in the way it was operated, when it opened for the 1958 season under Sid and Harry's control. With their mother having taken such a back seat through much of the 1950s, it really was a case of business as usual.

Sid, in particular, was a very well liked and extremely well respected member of Bridlington's amusement community. Geoff Gibson remembers his visits to Joyland as a child, when he managed to slip away from Bay View:

"If I went into Joyland and he saw me, he used to give me a five bob bag of copper. 'Sixty pennies to go and play on his machines', he used to say, 'spend them in my place'."

Harry was also well known across the town and was famous for being a big man, with a big personality, always smoking a big cigar. He was also known as a very nice chap, but he could be unpleasant if he was crossed, his short temper showing through his kindly exterior. Employees of Pleasureland remember him regularly picking up a duster and throwing it into the middle of the arcade because something had upset him.

One of Harry's big loves was his dog, a black poodle called Satan. He had trained Satan to do amazing circus-style tricks, which he was always happy to demonstrate to his friends. But just like his mother, his biggest love was horse racing, and he would regularly go to the races in York and elsewhere, where his own horses, Burlington Boy and Cheb's Lad (winner of the 1967 Champagne Stakes), would often race. He lived and breathed horse racing, more so than Sid, and loved nothing better than to talk about horses over a drink. He also had a slot machine called the Derby, and a couple of the horses in that machine were named after his.

Although Harry was rarely seen inside Joyland, he would often visit after a good day at the races. He would come back in a good mood, having been on the champagne. Although he was a large man, when he had a good day at the races, he was game for anything. One of his favourite tricks was trying to 'jump' the Chariot Racer ride.

It was well known in the town that Sid really took on the lion's share of the work. Joyland was his life. Many staff and visitors from this period remember that Sid would always sit on a stool, smartly dressed, cigar in mouth, right in the centre of the arcade, where he could see most of the complex, just as he had done when his mother was still alive. In fact, the staff always used to joke that he would be buried there. He quite literally spent most of every day in that place, watching over his beloved arcade.

Harry lived on-site at Joyland, in the flat above the Esplanade entrance, which had also been his mother's home. Most of the rooms above the Esplanade entrance were disused or used for storage, but Harry's living quarters were palatial. It had a large, beautifully decorated ballroom, which Harry would use for parties. Visitors would comment that the flat was more like a country mansion than a flat above an amusement arcade.

Sid and Harry would spend many of their evenings in the County Club on Marlborough Terrace. This was a private members club, formed in 1926, which was frequented by the town's amusement caterers. It was a very traditional

Joyland's Esplanade entrance c.1960. Note the coffee stall selling 'Espresso Coffee'. In this period, Joyland could maximise sales from the frontage as the adjacent properties had not added canopies. Also on this frontage is an ice cream stall and bingo.
Robert Brown

place; to be able to drink in the Club, one had to be proposed and seconded. When the arcades closed at nine or ten o'clock at night, the amusement caterers would all go to the County Club, where they could drink and gamble.

Boom Town

The late 1950s and early 1960s were good years for Bridlington and for Joyland. Special trains were chartered to the town every weekend through the summer, loaded with people from places like Leeds, Wakefield, York, Doncaster and Nottingham. The trains would drop people off at one o'clock in the afternoon, and take them back at about six o'clock in the evening. It was a busy time.

Sid and Harry had taken control just as the industry was about to go through a big change, with the passing of the Betting & Gaming Act 1960, which finally legitimised gaming machines and made betting shops legal. The Act sought to liberalise the law on gaming so as to allow those who wanted to play for money to do so. It introduced the concept of a 'game of chance', in which prizes could be awarded by automatic machines for reasons other than skill alone. Until this Act was introduced, slot machines had to be either 'for amusement only' or – if there was to be a prize – had to include an element of skill. Games which gave prizes based on chance alone were not permitted. Following the introduction of the 1960 Act, a new type of automatic machine immediately superseded a whole era of slot machine technology, leaving traditional machines largely defunct. From this point onwards the 'for amusement only' Allwin machines, which had been so popular in Joyland for over a quarter of a century, started to disappear and be replaced by fruit machines with the promise of a payout.

In this new era for Joyland, Sid continued to be supported in the day-to-day running of the complex by Jack Henry, with Walter Hoyes heading up the team of mechanics. Harry had his own manager for Pleasureland, a man by the name of Douglas Perriss. He would drive Harry around in his Rolls Royce, and he would take him to the races. Douglas was, like Hoyes, something of a jack of all trades; an engineer who was also able to undertake building and electrical works.

This juvenile roundabout was located close to the Promenade entrance to Joyland. Reg Spencer

A general view of the Joyland complex close to the Promenade entrance. The juvenile roundabout can be seen to the right.

Reg Spencer

Joyland was still dominated by amusement machines. The Dodgem track took centre stage, and the Chariot Racer ark ride was in the open yard. The Monkey House had been removed by the early 1960s and replaced by more slot machines. At the Promenade end of the arcade was a popular attraction: the Winchester rifle range. By the Promenade entrance was a café, and along the opposite wall a row of Bally Gold Award machines ('Bally Bandits'). These had glass cabinets above them with the prizes displayed.

A new children's roundabout replaced the old one at the Promenade entrance. A Wurlitzer jukebox was also installed there, linked to all the speakers throughout Joyland. A visitor of the period, Terry Waddington, remembers how popular the jukebox was:

The Brown family c.1960: left to right, Carole, Peter, Margaret, Sidney, Harry and Robert.
Robert Brown

> *"In the 1950s, there was a jukebox just inside the front door to the Promenade. Jukeboxes were a new phenomenon in those days. At the weekends, all the local teenage lotharios, including myself, would congregate there to meet the visiting girls from the West Riding. One or two actually ended up getting married. Frankie Lane and Johnny Ray, etc, were our favourites. We used to feed the machine and would spend hours there."*

By the early 1960s, Sid's sons, Peter and Robert, were young men and were taking an increasingly active role in running the business, just as Sid and Harry had done a generation before. Peter left school in the late 1950s and started his Joyland career by doing the simple tasks, working his way up the ladder. One of his early jobs was weighing money on the potato scales. As his responsibilities increased, he showed great promise and by the mid-1960s he was manager of Little Joyland.

Peter's younger brother, Robert, joined the family business later, also starting at the bottom of the ladder. Early responsibilities were tea making, giving out change, key holding and money counting. One of the tasks that Robert did not relish was sweeping the floor:

> *"In those days there were no carpets. It was all concrete. And there was a certain way to mop concrete. The dust was everywhere. I can always remember dad showing people when they first came to work there. You had to flick water down to keep the dust down. In those days there was about 28,000 sq ft of floor, and it was mopped every morning an hour before we opened."*

Peter remembers how his father had insisted they learn on the job:

> *"Just because I was the son of the boss didn't mean I started at the top! They were very strict on making us start at the bottom and working up, doing all the jobs that had to be done, so that in time when we were instructing other people to do these jobs, we knew exactly how it should be done."*

However, Peter and Robert were not always welcome recipients of their father's guiding hand. One thing they found difficult was starting at eight o'clock, especially when at the neighbouring Bay View arcade, Raymond Gibson's son, Geoff, started a whole hour later.

In the foreground is a coin-operated 'table football' game. Behind can be seen a row of Gold Award machines, with cabinets full of prizes above. Tokens won from the machines could be exchanged for the prizes.

Reg Spencer

One day they decided to confront their father on this subject. Robert did the talking: "I don't think it is fair. In the middle of winter we have to come down and start at eight o'clock, and Geoff working for his dad doesn't have to start until nine." Sid had a very straight answer to that question: "Yes, but when Geoff goes to work at nine o'clock, he starts work. When you and Peter come to work at eight o'clock, it takes you an hour to get that bloody fire lit to make your bloody cup of coffee. You never get started until nine in any case!"

Changing Attractions in the 1960s

Another new attraction to hit Joyland in this period was bingo. The game of bingo as we know it today had started life in the USA in the 1930s as a fairground game called 'Beans'. In Britain, bingo had begun in the Second World War, when British servicemen played it on troopships (at this time it was known as 'housey housey'). It was the 1960s when bingo started to appear in amusement arcades around the UK. The combination of the 1960 Betting & Gaming Act, plus the social changes and relative affluence of the period, brought about a speedy expansion of the game. It was at this time when it first appeared in Joyland, an arcade that was always willing to experiment with new ideas. Early bingo was very basic; the Browns used to ask several of the local pubs to save bottle tops, which they used as the markers. It wasn't long, however, before bottle tops were replaced with electronics and bingo became the game we all know today.

Other technological innovations were introduced into the amusement industry in this period. Firstly, money-counting machines saved a great deal of time. Then came automated change machines for the change desks. All the Joyland change desks were fitted out with machines that would issue the correct money just by the press of a button.

Before this innovation, it had been a time consuming job to prepare the money. The first job in the morning for the cashiers was to cover the change desk in piles of pennies laid out a shilling high. Then they would get a piece of card, put it on top, and start all over again building shilling-high piles. This enabled the cashiers to be prepared for the rush.

One distinctive feature of Joyland was the coloured lights along the top of every wall; there were quite literally thousands of them. Ordering the bulbs was one of the jobs given to Peter Brown. The Dodgem area was also re-themed in this period with a distinctive rock/stonework effect, which would last into the 1980s, and came to characterise the central part of Joyland. The effect was created from a mixture of chicken wire, concrete and wood, and painted in shades of green to give it a realistic rock-like appearance.

In 1969, Joyland took the very expensive step of replacing all of its Dodgem cars, which had run continuously since the 1930s, much longer than their expected life span (thanks, no doubt, to Walter Hoyes' love and attention). In the same year, they also added new coloured lighting around the Dodgems and extended it around some of the building. Some stalls were updated, whilst other out of date stalls were demolished and replaced with new, electrically operated machines.

Walter Hoyes remembers this as being the pinnacle of Joyland's success:

"The remaining years of the 1960s saw little change in the arcade. Occasionally, a new machine would be installed, but to me it was the busiest, and sometimes the most stressful period, of the time I was there."

Towards the end of Sid and Harry's reign, 'coin pushers' began to appear in arcades, and would become hugely popular machines, dominating arcades until the advent of video games, but still remaining a major part of the amusement arcade scene. The attraction of these machines is quite simple. Coins get pushed ever closer to the edge of a payout chute,

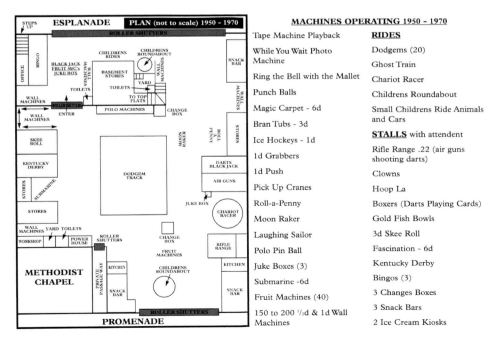

Plan of Joyland as it appeared in the 1950s and 1960s, before its expansion in the late 1970s.

Walter Hoyes

JOYLAND
BRIDLINGTON

BROADER & SPENCER

5, BRIDGE STREET, YORK YO1 1DE

(OPPOSITE BOYES) TELEPHONE No. 59346 (4 LINES)

ALSO AT
1, BOOTHAM, EXHIBITION SQUARE, YORK , TEESSIDE, BURNLEY, BURY, NELSON & COLNE.

In the early 1970s, Sid and Harry Brown decided to retire and put Joyland on the market. A brochure was produced, but the complex was eventually taken off the market and would remain in the Brown family for several more years.

Reg Spencer

eventually teetering precariously over the edge – will the next coin be the one to push them over? Pushers were the biggest revolution in slot machines since the demise of the Allwins ten years earlier.

In 1970, Sid and Harry hit upon the idea of opening Pleasureland all year round. Until that time, both Joyland and Pleasureland had closed in September, and had not reopened until Easter. Because Pleasureland was right in the town centre, they thought it could operate as if it were a shop, providing entertainment for locals outside of the holiday season. The 1970 experiment was a great success and the following year they decided to extend the experiment to Joyland. They considered that the Esplanade end was too far from the town centre to be viable, and the outdoor areas would be too cold in the winter. They therefore decided to open the Promenade part of the complex, but kept the open yard area closed so that the arcade would be warm. This too was a big hit with the people of the town, and Joyland would remain open all year from this point onwards.

By the early 1970s, Peter and Robert were both much more involved in the running of the arcade, like their father had been when their grandmother was alive. Peter was by now in charge of the Bingo, looking after the ordering order of prizes and the accounts.

A significant personnel change in this period was the retirement of Walter Hoyes in May 1970, after 20 years with the Browns, leaving the arcade without a Chief Engineer. Perhaps Hoyes' retirement seemed like the end of an era for the brothers, but it wasn't long after he left the arcade that Sid and Harry made a surprising decision: they decided to put Joyland up for sale. Local agents Broader and Spencer were instructed, and they put together a fine brochure, which stated: "We are favoured to offer this fabulous amusement park on instructions from Messrs Harry and Sidney Brown, who after a lifetime in the business are retiring." It was described as a "unique opportunity to acquire one of the finest and well known leisure parks on the East Coast".

The description of Joyland by the estate agents was first-rate:

"Carefully planned and laid out in so much detail, the arcade enjoys one of the most sought after trading positions on the sea front in this popular coastal resort. So well sited to attract visitors, in Bridlington's main Promenade thoroughfare, immediately opposite the Bus Station and extending almost 100 yards in through depth to open out with a magnificent frontage to Esplanade, to overlook the North Sands and Sea Front yet have the advantage of linking two important town centre thoroughfares, both routes attracting the multitude of visitors to enjoy the amenities of this fine coastal resort."

The brochure also provided a wonderful description of the inside of the complex and a list of some of the main attractions at that time:

> *"A Ground Floor layout in almost 28,000 square feet is enhanced by the colourful décor and magnificent array of multi-coloured lighting, whilst the central Supercar Dodgem Track, Rifle Range, Bingo, Snack Bar, children's roundabouts and a host of pintables, fruit machines and a vast selection of other entertainment features make this one of the most notable, active and well-patronised pleasure parks."*

The Joyland Bingo in full swing.

Reg Spencer

A view of Promenade in 1972, with Joyland clearly visible on the right. Over the next few years, an array of signs would be added to he façade, culminating in a massive illuminated sign for the 1980 season.

Charlie Chinnery

The brochure even touched upon Joyland's long family heritage:

"Joyland has been in the same family hands for over 35 years and even with its abundance of pleasure and arrangement of machines in the most vantageous [sic] positions there is a feeling of spaciousness with the whole of the layout so expertly arranged to allow for free access and movement. The premises also incorporate a spacious luxury flat and two three-storey residences ideal for other conversions."

Although interest was shown in the complex, Sid and Harry eventually decided not to sell. Joyland was to remain in the ownership of the Brown family and was about to enter a new phase of development.

Other arcades in the 1960s and early 1970s

In this photograph from the 1960s, showman John Ling had opened an arcade in the former Lounge Cinema café and foyer. He would eventually acquire Bay View to create the largest amusement arcade frontage on Esplanade.
Geoff Gibson

By the 1960s, amusement arcades were still springing up in Bridlington. In 1961, the Lounge Cinema, located between Joyland and Bay View, finally closed. The Esplanade cinema foyer and cafe was sold as a separate property. Surprisingly, it was not Bay View or Joyland that bought it. A travelling fairground operator called John Ling, one of the most successful showmen of the 20th Century, opened a small amusement arcade in the former foyer, having decided to enter the still burgeoning amusement arcade business. Ling had begun looking at sites for a possible permanent amusement arcade the previous year and it was whilst open with a Waltzer in Withernsea during the summer of 1962 that he became aware that the Lounge was available. Ling's arcade opened for the 1963 season.

In 1964, Albert Corrigan and his family arrived, and opened amusements on Esplanade near to Joyland. Albert had decided to stop travelling and become a 'flattie' (the term used in the world of showpeople when a showman decides to give up travelling).

But the town's second Corrigan arcade didn't open without a fight. Corrigans were the first amusement caterers in Bridlington to take on the might of the Local Planning Authority and go to appeal. To open an amusement arcade on Esplanade, Albert Corrigan would have

to acquire a shop unit and convert it to amusement use. Unfortunately, the Council refused planning permission to convert the shops into amusements, the argument being that Bridlington had enough amusement arcades. Corrigans took the appeal to a public inquiry and won. The Council saw that as opening the floodgates to amusements all along Esplanade. The Corrigans are still represented on Bridlington Esplanade to this day, albeit now in a different unit, but in many ways the Council's predictions were right. The floodgates had been opened, and Bay View and Joyland were joined by numerous other arcades up and down the seafront. By 1999, most of the Esplanade was amusement arcades, but the Council could not have predicted at that time how much they would add to the appeal of the resort.

One year later, in the summer of 1965, Charlie Walker's Corner Bingo (later known as the Harbour

Charles and Joan Walker of Harbour Top Amusements at a Showmen's Guild of Great Britain event in London, circa 1955.
Wes Walker

Top Amusements) opened on the corner of Prince Street and Garrison Street. Walker was himself an amusement arcade pioneer. He was among the very first to bring bingo games off the showgrounds and into resort premises. He relocated permanently to Bridlington but retained business interests in his native Leeds. His arcade was leased from showman Norman Aveyard until the Walkers were certain of its future as a "live one". Prior to that, it had been 'Murphy's' for years, the sign emblazoned across the brickwork.

The Walker family resided for some 15 years in the floors above the bingo hall in Harbour House, which had stock rooms placed midway between landings. The cellars consisted of two separate rooms, one a long passageway emerging under the harbour itself, but always kept locked. This old smuggler's passage acted as a storage area for old rides, which only emerged from their underground cavern each year for Hull Fair.

Despite the newcomers, Bay View still remained Joyland's biggest competitor. Although it wasn't as big as Joyland, it now had an equally large frontage, so was still able to attract considerable numbers through its entrance. In the 1960s, it was still run by Raymond Gibson, but his son, Geoffrey, was now heavily involved.

Sid and Harry Brown both became good friends with Raymond Gibson during the 1960s, when they were – between them – the three most powerful people in the town's tourism industry. Sid Brown had always made Geoff Gibson

Charlie Walker's Bingo and The Royal Mint, drawn by Wes Walker.
Wes Walker

Bay View in the 1960s with its new-look sign.
Geoff Gibson

In the 1960s, the toy stall had been replaced by an ice cream stall. This was reputedly the most popular ice cream stall on Bridlington seafront.
Geoff Gibson

welcome in Joyland. In later years, Harry Brown and Raymond Gibson became partners in the ownership of racehorses.

As the 1960s moved towards the 1970s, changes were afoot at Bay View. Still a popular arcade, it had a wide range of machines, stalls, and – just like Joyland – included bingo. By 1971, Raymond Gibson was nearing retirement age. His involvement in the arcade was slowly reducing year on year. He had bought a bungalow in the Norfolk Broads and he and his wife Dorothy were spending more time there. He had suffered two heart attacks by this time, and finally decided that he was no longer able to continue operating the arcade. It was an agonising decision for Raymond, as the arcade had been his life, and that of his father. His son, Geoff Gibson, was by now very involved in the running of the arcade, having worked there since leaving school in 1961. It seemed natural to Raymond to ask his son if he wanted to take over the running of the arcade. To Raymond's surprise, his son refused. Geoff Gibson explains:

> "*In those days in that arcade we would employ up to 50 people, although most were on a part time basis. That was a lot of people, and I should imagine that Joyland probably employed as many as well, if not more. It was a headache to keep the place going. There were always people not turning up. It was a difficult business to run, and you were open long hours. You were open from ten in the morning until ten at night, so you were doing 12 hour days, seven days a week. My father had also suffered two heart attacks at that time. So, I said no to him: 'If you want to sell it, you sell it. You retire'.*"

So Bay View was put on the market and it was not long before a buyer had been found. The buyer was John Ling. His strategic acquisition of The Lounge foyer had meant that he had inserted himself between Joyland and Bay View, preventing either arcade from acquiring the other, should they come on the market. Whether by accident or design, he had secured himself a prominent position in Bridlington's tourism industry, almost overnight. By extending

Inside South Cliff Amusements in the early 1970s. Typical of arcades of the period, it was open fronted, but this arcade featured a distinctive crazy paving floor! At the entrance are the ubiquitous children's rides and one-arm bandits. In the background can be seen Streets 'Wheel 'Em In'.

Geoff Gibson

Geoff Gibson, grandson of two Bridlington amusement arcade giants: Percy Firth (Luna Park/Joyland) and William Gibson (Bay View). Geoff operated South Cliff Amusements until 2003, when the arcade was sold to John Noble. Geoff Gibson

his small operation into the vast Bay View site, he created the largest amusement frontage in Bridlington. Almost immediately he introduced sweeping changes, the first being the demolition of the old cottage behind the arcade, which at the time was still being used as a workshop.

Following the sale, Geoff Gibson turned his attentions to operating his father's other arcade, South Cliff Amusements, which he operated until 2003.

Another significant amusement arcade of the period was Carousel Amusements (8/9 Garrison Street). This was purchased in 1969 by Joan and Charles Walker (the owner of nearby Harbour Top Amusements). This was the most substantial property on the Garrison Street block, once the adjoining amusement arcades had been downsized by several storeys following bomb damage from the wartime hits taken by Woolworths and the Cock & Lion Hotel. In 1972, its name was changed to 'Casino Royale'. Brian Walker's son, Wes Walker, remembers it well:

"Upstairs, Casino Royale was a veritable warren – a disused maze of once glorious hotel layout. There were even half-begun adapted floors between storeys, as the ceilings were so high they could accommodate it. These 'floors' were accessible only by jumping midway from a staircase onto a haphazard stack of steps arranged like a landing stage. At the very foot of a half-remaining staircase were two hatches leading into a room consisting of the upside of the illuminated ceiling of the arcade! It appeared like the discotheque floor of Saturday Night Fever!"

"When we took it over with the last vestiges of a vast restaurant across the first floor, the cellars were stocked high with the apparent quantity of crockery and catering equipment pertaining to an army commissary."

The Late Sid and Harry Years

Harry Brown lived in the flat above Joyland's Esplanade entrance throughout his years in control of Joyland and Pleasureland. Sid had also lived in the flat, but once he had got married he moved out and bought a house at the Sandsacre Estate. In his later years, Harry became more and more of a recluse. He had developed diabetes, and his nurse, Eileen Lenderyou, remembers visiting his flat above the amusements on many occasions:

Brian Walker in early summer 1978 outside Walkers Tussauds Waxworks, Royal Prince's Parade. Wes Walker

"To get to his seafront apartment one had to go into the arcade and up a narrow flight of stairs. As the summer progressed, each side of the steps got higher – piled up with over-filled bags of money! By the end of the summer, one had to actually walk on the bags of coins to get up and down the stairs to the flat".

Eileen was very concerned that, being a very large man, he might be putting himself in danger by climbing down the stairs. She therefore voiced her concern. "Oh, not to worry", he said, "they will soon be gone. All these bags contain bent and damaged coins. To make sure that they don't go back into the machines we keep them bagged up and send them to the bank at the end of the season. They will all be gone when you come next time."

Bingo win vouchers from Casino Royale on Garrison Street (note the incorrect spelling of Royale!) and Harbour Top Amusements on Prince Street.
Wes Walker

On 24th May 1972 Harry died suddenly in Scarborough Hospital, aged 65. Although he was not a fit man, his death came as a great shock to all the family. The funeral took place at Bridlington Cemetery, following a service in the Church of Our Lady and St. Peter.

His obituary in the Bridlington Free Press of 2nd June 1972, remembered him as more than just an amusement caterer:

> *"He was a popular character among northern racegoers, he was the owner of Chebs Lad, winner of the Champagne Stakes at Doncaster and several other major races. Burlington Boy, one of a string of horses owned by him and trained at Malton by Snowy Wainwright, has been named as the best two-year-old seen in the North this year."*

It was not long after Harry's death that Sid too fell ill and his doctor broke the news that he was not going to recover. On hearing this, he knew that there was one thing that he just had to do. He was already arranging to pass the Joyland/Pleasureland businesses on to his two sons, Peter and Robert, but he wanted to be able to pass them the freehold ownership of Pleasureland as well. He contacted the Southcott family, made them an offer, and that same day the deal was agreed. Pleasureland was to be taken over by the Browns, almost 35 years after they had turned it into one of the town's most popular amusement centres. The arcade passed immediately into the ownership of Peter and Robert Brown in the summer of 1972.

Casino Royale amusement arcade on Garrison Street circa 1984, by Wes Walker. Wes Walker

Margaret and Sidney Brown. Robert Brown

Sidney Brown died on 22nd August 1972 in a Hull nursing home, aged 62. A funeral service was held at the Roman Catholic Church of Our Lady and St. Peter on Friday 25th August. Peter Brown remembers that night as being particularly painful:

"On the very night Dad died there was a fire in the Joyland snack bar fronting Promenade. It was only the quick response of the local fire brigade that saved the whole arcade from burning down. The snack bar was destroyed, but it could have been so much worse. What a night! Dad died and Joyland almost went up in flames!"

View of the Esplanade entrance in 1970. 'The Largest Amusement Centre in the Town' boasts a sign above the canopy.

Reg Spencer

View of the Promenade entrance in 1970. Note the lights on the turrets and signs advertising the 'Winchester Range' and 'Dodgem Cars Inside'.

Reg Spencer

NINE

Peter and Robert Brown: Joyland Amusement Park

"As a boy, I absolutely worshipped the guys who collected the Dodgem money as the cars were in motion. It was my life's ambition to hop from one car to the other, hand outstretched under the driver's noses for the 'brass', in that nonchalant, casual way, while holding onto the electric pole with the other."

CHRIS YOUHILL

Joyland's Esplanade entrance in all its glory. The small crowd gathered under the 'Joyland' sign is watching a sale in the 'Bridlington & Scarborough Bargain Centre', a short-lived retail experiment in Joyland. Jim Dodgson

At the time of their father's death, Peter and Robert were both very involved in the running of the business and were able to take over immediately. Sid's insistence on the two brothers starting from the bottom and learning on the job had paid off.

Straight away they introduced changes, the first of which was to introduce uniforms for the staff, to give a smart, unified appearance.

Peter and Robert decided now was the time to introduce better working conditions for employees, in an attempt to reduce the high turnover of staff. They decided to let the senior staff have a day off, provided it was not Saturday or Sunday, and others were allowed an afternoon and evening off. This was the first time that Joyland staff had not worked the full seven days.

Taking over the running of Joyland was not an entirely easy ride. The duties from the deaths of Sid and Harry were enormous. At one point the brothers even thought that they might have had to sell Pleasureland to pay the duties. However, there was a solution available to them to reduce the level of investment, whilst ensuring that the arcade changed with the times.

Until Peter and Robert took over, everything inside Joyland was owned by the family. But now, when an old machine broke down, or went out of fashion, Peter and Robert did not replace it. Instead, they rented the space it occupied to machine operators.

It was also soon after Peter and Robert took over that amusement machines began to change. Slowly at first, slot machines began to change from mechanical to electronic, but it wasn't long after the brothers had taken over that the big video machine craze began.

Working as a Team

Peter and Robert knew that they needed a good team to run Joyland. They had big plans for the place, but could not do it alone. They were supported by some great characters, some who had been with the arcade for many years.

Jack Henry was still working in Joyland as he had for Sid and Harry, and Charlotte before that, still acting as General Manager. Jack was a fascinating, eccentric character and somebody who knew the practical side of the business probably better than anybody. He could turn his hand to most things, from managing the staff to repairs and electrical work. Because he was related to Charlotte, and had been with the Company for so long, he was well trusted and given a lot of responsibility. He was also well-known in the town for his large collection of 'bubble cars', which filled his garden, some even buried.

Whilst Jack Henry continued to be invaluable, one person who was sorely missed was Walter Hoyes. Indeed, they had noticed that the place was not being run as efficiently since his retirement. They decided that they needed a permanent, senior member of staff, someone who could keep his eye on both the mechanics and the machines, and ensure that the place ran smoothly and efficiently. But efficiency was not the only reason. The change to electronic machines had, quite frankly, meant that many of their senior staff, including Jack Henry, were being left behind by technology. What they needed was their own Walter Hoyes, someone who could deal with everything that was thrown at him by fast-developing technology.

They remembered that their father had employed a man called Ronald Walls, who was a highly experienced amusement machine mechanic. Ronald had experience of this type of machine from his time with electronic machine hire firm, Music Hire, and the Browns knew that they needed a man of his talents. He had only been with Joyland for a short while, but left in a dispute over wages. However, Peter and Robert knew that they would need the best, so they got in touch with him. Luckily for them, Ronald accepted, and was soon back on the payroll as Chief Engineer.

Ronald took on two further mechanics as apprentices: Derek Taylor and Steve Honour. Both of these were self-taught, and they supported Ronald, servicing the amusement machines.

They also experimented with different uses for the small, isolated unit fronting Esplanade. For many years it was a small arcade, but Peter and Robert decided to open the notorious 'Knock-Down Shop'. Joyland mechanic Derek Taylor remembers it very well:

> *"At 11.00 or 11.30 in the morning there would be a crowd in the room, with a platform at the back. This geezer would produce something, put it on this counter, and say, 'I'm not here today and gone tomorrow. I'm selling this. Who would have one?'*
> *And it is something in a bag, and you don't know what is in it. Fools would just pay him, and he had the gift of the gab. The police were always there, as you can imagine."*

Chief Engineer Ronald Walls pictured in the Workshop.

Ronald Walls

Eventually, the Knock-Down Shop was closed, partly because it was damaging the family image of Joyland. Peter and Robert then tried out other ideas in this unit, including a juvenile roundabout and a modern themed shooting gallery, the Hillbilly Moonshine.

Shortly after the installation of the shooting gallery, Robert Brown holidayed in Las Vegas and returned with the idea of creating a little bit of the Vegas Strip in Joyland. This small unit would be the site of an experiment. A new amusement arcade was created that resembled a Vegas casino. Wood panelling and chandeliers were installed, and 'Slots A Fun', as it was called, became the first part of Joyland to be carpeted. Whilst this small arcade was successful, Browns did not roll out the format across the rest of Joyland.

New Rides, New Ideas

Peter and Robert were keen to update Joyland's rides, and make the place work as much as an amusement park as an arcade. Ultimately, within a few short years, they would completely transform Joyland, turning it into a major regional attraction. One of their first decisions was to remove the ageing Chariot Racer ride, which had been in Joyland since 1952. Peter and Robert remembered how popular the original Ghost Train had been in this location, so decided that the Chariot Racer would be replaced for the 1973 season by a new one. This would be the first ride the brothers had ever bought and they would learn a lot from the experience.

The brothers visited a trade show in London and, as they walked around, they were intrigued by the stand of one of the leading ride builders of the day, Supercar (the company which made the Joyland Dodgem cars). They spoke to Supercar's Mr Webb about the possibility of purchasing a new Ghost Train – not a small travelling ride, but a full-size 'dark ride' designed for amusement parks. It wasn't long before the Browns had signed on the dotted line.

Supercar proved extremely efficient. They quickly assembled the ride in the area formerly occupied by the Chariot Racer and it wasn't long before the day came for the brothers to ride their Ghost Train.

Excitedly, they boarded one of the new cars and slammed through the swing doors , starting their journey into darkness. After a few seconds, Robert turned to Peter and said, "Where are the effects?" A few seconds later, the ride had finished, and the brothers got out. There had been no moving models, no sounds, and no lighting effects. In fact, it was quite literally a ride in complete darkness and complete silence! They were quickly on the telephone to Supercar, who confirmed to them that what they had bought was, quite literally, a 'dark ride', and that there were no effects. "It is sold as a dark ride, we do not sell effects," said the Supercar representative. The idea was that an amusement park would buy the ride – building, track, and cars – and then theme it as required: a fantasy fairytale ride, a Ghost Train, whatever the park wanted. Suddenly it all made sense. Robert and Peter's inexperience had led them to buy a dark room!

For the 1974 season, the Browns added a helter skelter. This was operated by a concessionaire, Edward Sheeran (of Sheeran Amusements, Lanarkshire), and was another part of the Browns' approach of allowing different operators into the complex to widen the variety of attractions, and boost visitor numbers. The Browns had a big surprise when they woke up at Spring Bank Holiday Sunday, ready to open the new ride to the holiday crowd, only to find the helter skelter covered top to bottom in snow. The Browns and their staff set to work shovelling the snow from the yards so that people could walk from one part of the arcade to the other. The helter skelter only remained for one season.

Kentucky Derby

A new attraction was installed in Joyland for the 1975 season, which would see a new face in the arcade, a man who would play a major role in the future development of the business. Leeds-based Stuart Keane was a flamboyant character, and his ideas and enthusiasm were to change Joyland more than it had ever changed before.

Stuart Keane had been brought up in the amusement business. His father was an operator of fruit machines, and by 18 years of age, Stuart was selling his father's fruit machines. This would take him to arcades all around the country, and once in the 1950s it took him to a certain Bridlington establishment:

> *"I did actually meet Charlotte Brown once. I went into Joyland to try and sell her some equipment, but I wasn't successful. That was as a young lad. She was sharp, very sharp. There were a lot of women in the business like that at the time. "*

In a space-leasing deal with the Browns, the first attraction he installed was the Kentucky Derby, which was introduced in 1975.

The Kentucky Derby was a group competitive game, where players rolled their balls into a set of target holes to power their racing horse and hopefully win the race. The first and original Kentucky Derby game was introduced in the 1940s by an American jockey, G V Tonner, and was sited on Blackpool sea front for a number of years. When Stuart Keane came into the picture, the Derby was being manufactured by Elton Fabrications (now Elton Games plc) of Southport. Elton Fabrications had been formed in 1962 by Arthur Helm, whose father had operated one of the first Derbys at Southport's Pleasureland Amusement Park. His intention was to manufacture an English version of the game for the home market. Elton built its first Derby in 1972, which was sold to an amusement park in New Brighton.

In Joyland, the Derby replaced what was called Fascination, which was an area of the arcade made up of little alcoves, inside each of which was a wall machine, of the type that had been popular in Joyland from the 1930s. By the early 1970s, wall-mounted slot machines were losing popularity, and the area had effectively fallen into disuse, not helped by the fact that it was partly hidden behind the Dodgems. It needed a new anchor attraction to pull people into this difficult part of the arcade.

Keane remembers those first hours in Joyland:

> *"I took the 12-player Derby over in a Transit Van. It was a Thursday when I started building up. There was nobody else there and it was freezing. It took me all day. At about half-past nine or half past ten at night I finished. I had no digs. I went outside in the thick of snow, and I got some digs round the corner. I went back the next day and it wasn't a very good opening. It was Good Friday and there was nobody around. It was snowing and I remember Robert saying, 'If the weather is half-decent on Monday, don't worry. You'll have a good day. Don't worry. Don't worry. We always have these bad days.' I thought, 'What have I done here?' When I went looking for digs I felt like Mary must have felt like. No room at the inn. There were no vacancies, and it was snowing sideways. Robert said, 'Sometimes it can take you 20 minutes to walk from the front of the arcade to my office.' And, he was right. It was very rare for this to happen, but when it got busy, it did get busy! You couldn't move."*

Mechanic Derek Taylor pictured by Stuart Keane's Kentucky Derby in 1978.

Derek Taylor

Sale of Pleasureland

In 1978, the Brown family decided to sell Pleasureland. It was acquired by Chester-le-Street-based John Noble. Born in 1935, Noble was already a prominent amusement caterer in the north east of England, with a background on the travelling fairs. His two teenage sons, John and Jason, helped him run his arcades business. Noble embarked on a programme of modernisation of Pleasureland, which saw the ceilings lowered and glass doors installed, paving the way for the warm, luxurious amusement arcade of today. The Noble family would all later play a major role in the future of Joyland.

Peter and Robert had been offered a considerable amount of money for Pleasureland. For them, the timing was right; it meant they could now concentrate solely on Joyland, and it would help them realise the next phase of their ambitious expansion plans.

Joyland's Esplanade entrance pictured on a busy summer's day in 1978.

Nick Laister

New Ideas

The late 1970s was a time of major change. And whilst the Brown brothers would forge ahead with the development and expansion of Joyland, not all of their ideas were implemented.

The rooms above Joyland were all under-used. The rooms over the Promenade entrance were still in use as the Copper Room, where Jack Henry or Ronald Walls would weigh and bag

Robert Brown stands outside the Esplanade entrance of Joyland in the summer of 1978.
Peter and Linda Brown

coins. Other than the Counting Room, all the rooms over the Esplanade entrance had fallen out of use. The rooms were empty and partly derelict, with nothing more than the odd pile of bingo swag to break up the endless cobwebs and dust. Peter and Robert knew that there was potential to extend Joyland onto these upper floors, so they decided to apply for planning permission to reopen these floors as a public house.

They secured planning permission in September 1978 but they could not get a license. Robert remembers:

> *"The licensing magistrate said, 'You can't have a pub up above. Children are going to get out of the amusements and they are going to get into the pub.'"*

Undaunted, the Browns re-applied, this time for a licensed restaurant, which they believed would overcome the issue. Planning permission was granted for the restaurant in November 1978, but the permission was never implemented. By this time, they had already turned their attention back to the core business.

By the end of the 1978 season, Joyland's style of operation had changed significantly. Peter and Robert Brown had successfully introduced a number of concessionaires into the complex, reducing the amount of staff directly employed by Joyland itself by almost 50%. The September 1978 edition of Country Life reported on this much-changed attraction:

> *"Joyland has about 25 people in the height of the season and keeps ten on in winter for maintenance of the machines. They haven't quite so many as they used to have, as some of the attractions, such as the Kentucky Derby, are franchised to other entrepreneurs. But they need staff of their own, of course, which makes it a very big complex indeed, and one of the oldest in the fun business."*

The Last Waltzer

As the 1978 season drew to a close, the Browns embarked on the next stage of their redevelopment and modernisation programme, which would start to change Joyland more than it had ever been changed before. The idea was to tackle a different part of the building each year.

After its first few seasons of operation, the Ghost Train had proved itself as a hugely successful ride. Clearly, the appetite was there for bigger, better rides, so the brothers decided to replace an area of slot machines with a new ride. If this worked, they could continue the concept elsewhere in the arcade. They decided that the only way they could grow Joyland in this capital-intensive way was to start franchising parts of the arcade off. This would undoubtedly pay off for the Browns' own equipment (from the slot machines right up to the Ghost Train and Dodgems) by bringing more people into the arcade. But they didn't want to just rent the space as many amusement parks do (and as they had done themselves with the helter skelter and Kentucky Derby), they wanted to be a part of any new operation on a joint venture basis, so that they could retain some sort of quality control and could reap more of the rewards. It also worked for them because, unlike most amusement parks, which are effectively just an area of open land, to install rides in Joyland would often mean physical works to the fabric of the building – it was therefore essential that they were directly involved in the projects.

Their approach was to supply the site free of charge, on the condition that the operator provides the equipment free of charge, and they would each take a share of the proceeds. But before they could start, they needed to find an operator of fairground rides who had the same passion for the business as they had. They found this person in the form of Stuart Keane, who had introduced the Kentucky Derby into Joyland in 1975.

Stuart Keane was certain that the first new ride should be a waltzer, one of the most popular rides to be found in fairgrounds and amusement parks at that time, a well-known further development of the roundabout, with spinning cars travelling on an undulating platform. He knew there would be a market for it as at the time there was no other waltzer in the town. But where in Joyland could it go? The only real space was in the part of Joyland known as 'The Centre', adjacent to the Dodgems. The area was measured up, but there was insufficient height to install the machine. A waltzer is raised to allow the motor to sit underneath the pay box in the centre of the ride. Because of these problems, Peter and Robert were convinced that it could not be done. Stuart remembers the challenge:

"It was a feat in itself because, in diameter, it was the smallest nine-car waltzer that had ever been made, because it had to fit in-between two uprights that were holding the upper storeys of the building up. There was also the height problem. If anybody stood up in the car as it went round, they would have hit their head on a crossbeam."

Mechanic Derek Taylor pictured in the open yard in 1979. Behind him is the legendary Joyland jukebox, where many romances began!

Derek Taylor

Stuart Keane had an idea: put it in a hole. The Browns agreed that it could be done, and they gave the go-ahead for Joyland's most ambitious project to date, and what would become the only waltzer on which you walk down steps to reach the platform.

Local architect John Board drew up the plans and to Stuart's delight he confirmed that the idea of sinking a waltzer into a pit would work. At the end of the 1978 season, the Bally Gold Awards electric fruit machines, which were located on the chosen site, were removed. In the depths of winter 1978, the builders came on site, and the hole for the waltzer was dug, five feet deep. The Bridlington Free Press of 10th May 1979 recalled the difficulties of getting a 45ft ride into such a small space:

> "It was decided to completely demolish the ground floor of an existing four-storey building and cover in an open yard area to provide the necessary space. This meant putting the existing building on stilts and involved a total of 21 steel girders being installed, some of which had to be specially cantilevered to ensure that none were within the area of the ride."

The staff all wondered what the hole was to be used for. Stuart had asked Peter and Robert not to tell them. He wanted to achieve maximum impact. It was assumed the hole must be for water, so they all formed the opinion that Joyland was about to launch a new water ride, probably with boats.

Then the big day came for the Waltzer to be delivered. Custom-built for Joyland by HP Jackson & Son Ltd of Congleton, Cheshire, it was supplied with no top as it was to be operated indoors. Joyland had arranged for traffic along the Esplanade to be stopped whilst the ride was delivered.

Peter Brown (left) and building consultant John Board sitting in a car on the new Disco Waltzer ride in 1979.
Peter and Linda Brown

Advert from the Bridlington Free Press on 12 April 1979, announcing the new Disco Waltzer ride, which opened on Good Friday. Nick Laister Collection.

The work was completed in time for an Easter 1979 opening. To mark the opening, the brothers put an advert in the Bridlington Free Press, incorporating a token for free rides. The Waltzer was an immediate smash hit; that first year the ride took a considerable amount of money.

The material dug out of the hole was used to create a raised area adjacent to the Waltzer called the Top Spot. This area had been a small yard between the two Esplanade entrances, which Peter and Robert arranged to be covered over. Joyland used its size to take advantage of the Space Invader craze that had swept the UK. The area was designed to be dark and space-themed, and included a huge collection of Space Invader machines, possibly the largest in the UK at the time.

Joyland's latest attraction, the indoor Disco Waltzer, shortly after construction was completed in 1979. Michael Smith

The Promenade frontage of Joyland in 1979, the building proudly advertising the 'Dodgem Cars', 'Ghost Train' and new 'Disco Waltzer'. Note the flags and extensive neon lighting, which ensured that Joyland dominated the street day and night.

Bridlington Free Press.

Mechanic Derek Taylor often helped out on the Waltzer in busy periods. He remembered one particular incident:

"They are very dangerous rides. I remember one Saturday, a local kid jumped on the back of one of the cars and grabbed hold of the back of the seat. This was just as the car was both spinning and rising to the crest of one of the hills. As the car went up the hill, it threw the kid straight off. I tell you, I thought he was going to be dead."

The Waltzer in July 1979. Behind can be seen the paybox of 'Browns Dodgems'.
Michael Smith

The gaff lads await riders on the Joyland Waltzer in July 1979. A ride on the Waltzer was 30p.
Michael Smith

Buying the Lounge Cinema

The next big change occurred in the winter of 1979/80. By this time, the remaining parts of the Lounge Cinema (the auditorium, the outbuildings, and the New Lounge restaurant fronting Promenade) were owned by local businessman Les Cowling. The former Palm Court was now in use as a restaurant, but the former cinema auditorium had fallen into disuse. Cowling had placed the auditorium and its outbuildings on the market.

Joyland's open yard, which in 1979 housed the Ghost Train, backed onto the auditorium. Although accessed from both Esplanade and Promenade, the Esplanade foyer entrance formed part of John Ling's amusement arcade. The main auditorium now, therefore, immediately abutted both Ling's and Joyland.

Peter and Robert Brown were understandably worried that the 'opposition' might buy it and extend. If John Ling were to buy it, he could extend into it and create a complex almost as big as Joyland. There was even the possibility that they could extend through to Promenade and create an attraction linking Esplanade to Promenade as Joyland did. They also realised that, if they were to acquire the cinema, this additional space would allow them to continue their strategy of introducing more rides without having to reduce the number of slot machines. They knew Les Cowling and decided to step in and buy it.

News of the expansion of Joyland's funfair into the Lounge did not cause a local outcry, but resulted in a letter from Surrey's Yvonne Arnaud Theatre in the Bridlington Free Press in August 1980, several months after the Cinema had been redeveloped:

> *"Having worked in Bridlington in theatre management and over the last 20 years in number one theatres throughout the country, I have always been amazed that whenever mention is made that the Floral Pavilion might be closed, there is a public outcry, yet for years local people have allowed the Lounge, one of the most beautiful small theatres in Yorkshire, to stay closed without a word.*
>
> > *"About two years ago, I was proud to be perhaps the last professional to tread the boards of this gem of a theatre whilst thinking if I might buy it, thus giving the town an intimate theatre in the centre, capable of housing summer shows and offering facilities out of season to local drama groups. Whilst the rest of the country are joining a save the theatres campaign, all I can say is shame on Bridlington people for forgetting this wonderful and beautiful theatre."*

Perhaps the lack of an outcry was due to the fact that, in 1980, Bridlington had two major operational theatres, the Spa Theatre and the 3B's.

As the cinema building had been disused for a number of years, it was an eerie place. Entering the building before the building works was like travelling in a time machine to the Victorian age, as everything had pretty much been left untouched. Being inside the old cinema alone could be an unnerving experience.

Joyland mechanic, Ronald Walls, had a memorable experience inside the old cinema. It was a Sunday in late 1979, shortly after it had been acquired by Joyland. Ronald and his wife were having dinner with Doug Perriss (the Pleasureland Manager) in the Lounge restaurant, which was separate to the main cinema auditorium, and was run by Roy Stamper for owner Les Cowling. On this day, Ronald witnessed the Grey Lady, a fabled ghost that was said to haunt the Lounge Cinema building. The Grey Lady is said to be the ghost of an actress, Mrs Gray, who is said to have hanged herself on the stage. Ronald takes up the story:

"You had to walk across a dance floor to get to the toilets, which were before you got into the old cinema. It was beautiful. It still had the old boxes on the wall. And I walked through, and I went into the toilet with no lights on. As I stood there in the dark, I just felt this 'thing'. I turned around and it was a hooded person in grey. It looked grey anyway. Even though it was pitch black, it had this aura of grey about it. It was a hooded person with a cloak on, and I presumed it would be a woman.

"I came out and Roy said to me, 'What's that? He looks like he has seen something?' I said. 'I've just seen this 'thing''. He said, 'Was it the Grey Lady?' Now, I hadn't said anything. Apparently it was a thespian from Victorian times."

The 1980 Season

To make way for a new open area created by the demolition of the former Lounge Cinema projection room and other outbuilldings, the Ghost Train was moved closer to the Esplanade entrance, effectively standing in a new open yard, on the site of the former cinema projection room. The area between the Ghost Train and Waltzer was roofed over.

Three new rides were brought in by Stuart Keane to fill the new open area and the cinema building itself:

- the Meteorite – a revolving cage that inclined to nearly vertical, whilst its riders were pinned to the cage by centrifugal forces;
- Cyclone Twist – a popular rotating ride, with the gondolas rotating in the opposite direction to the ride itself; and
- Coronation Ark/Speedway – similar to Joyland's former Chariot Racer ride, with riders sitting on animals (Ark) or motorbikes (Speedway).

Bringing the Meteorite into Joyland was the most difficult of all the tasks. This ride was manufactured new for Stuart Keane by Sam Ward. The ride was brought into the complex from

The Dodgem track was the centrepiece of Joyland for over 50 years. This picture shows the Supercar Dodgems in action. Note the rock-effect supports surrounding the track.
Reg Spencer

Esplanade. It was permanently mounted on the back of a lorry, and could not be removed. Therefore, the Passage (the main Esplanade entrance) had to be cleared to allow the lorry access through the arcade to the amusement park area. Stuart Keane remembers how difficult it was to get the Meteorite into its position:

"We had to take all the wheels off. It was down to the axles up. We got it in from the seafront, at the right hand side, and we had to winch it. We had to fasten it onto pillars and winch it. It was part of a lorry, and had its own engine that drove the ride. It was a feat of 'tugmanship', if you like, moving it this way, moving it that way. Changing positions where you were going to winch it from. They did a fantastic job. It was a great product, was the Meteorite."

Stuart and the Browns decided to install the Ark – Billy Manning's famous Coronation Ark, which Keane acquired from Clarence Pier Amusement Park in Southsea – in the former cinema auditorium. The Ark wasn't the first idea for the Cinema, though, as Stuart explains:

"We had to destroy the balcony to get the Ark in, which was a shame. I wanted to put the Ghost Train underneath the balcony. It would have fit. But the Browns wanted it in front-line position. It would have been better all-round, and wouldn't have made any difference in the takings of the Ghost Train. But it would have saved knocking the balcony down."

The Joyland Speedway was built by Lakins of Streatham in 1937 – one of the great pre-war ride builders – at a time when fairground was as popular with the public as it was ever going to get.

As fairground enthusiasts know, Speedways evolved from Ark rides (many being converted from one to another), which were fast undulating roundabouts featuring wooden animal figures. In many cases conversion to a Speedway simply involved exchanging animals for motorbikes.

The Joyland machine began life as the so-called 'Coronation Ark', built to celebrate the coronation of George VI. It was ordered by White Brothers of Barry Island for the Cosy Corner Amusement Park, which was run by William White.

In their day, Arks captured a public need for speed. Although a modern thrill ride, it also managed to capture the ornate style of the earlier switchbacks and fairground scenic railways (which were similar in many respects, but steam powered). The Coronation Ark featured lavish carved rails all around the ride, with carved false pillars and banisters capped with crowns. It also had huge 16-board extension fronts painted with Ben Hur scenes by leading fairground artist Edwin Hall. The extension was supported by 'ancient Briton' figures.

In 1942, Whites sold the ride to leading fairground showman Billy Manning. In 1947 he moved it to his Clarence Pier Amusement Park at Southsea, where cartoon-type scenes of American servicemen, depicting Britain at war, replaced the original Ben Hur décor. For the 1953 Coronation, Manning redecorated the ride, with Queen Elizabeth and Prince Philip.

Manning's Clarence Pier park and all of its rides were eventually acquired by showman Walter Shufflebottom, and the ride was put on the market. Stuart Keane and Robert Brown visited Southsea together to see it in 1980 and it moved to Joyland shortly afterwards.

The ride spent the early part of the season in its original paintwork, as fairground historian and World's Fair writer, Stephen Smith, remembers:

"I could hardly believe that the massive Lakin machine was going to open so close to home. It was, however, a huge disappointment as only a small portion was visible. The wonderful extension front was never built up because it was inside the cinema, and only two sections of the rounding boards were visible."

But, for fairground enthusiasts worse was to come, even though the ride retained its carved handrails, false pillars and Easyrider bikes. It was decided to re-theme the ride as a 'Disco Speedway', which meant painting it black and adding flashing Perspex disco lights.

Stuart Keane was less than thrilled by this development, as he remembers:

"I was very annoyed about that. I was over in the States and I telephoned to see if they were prepared for opening. I think it was Ray Clarke who asked if he could repaint the Speedway. So, I said, 'Fine. How much will it cost?' So he told me. I said, 'Oh, go ahead.' Of course, he painted it black. Luckily, because it was in a corner, only two thirds of it at the most got painted on the outside. And it was only done in water-based emulsion, so over the years it started to peal off, and you could see the original decoration, especially the artwork on the rounding boards and the shutters."

Due to the slope in the floor it had to be partly on blocks to level it. As it was designed as a travelling ride, and was not fixed to the ground, when the ride operated in the cinema the vibration was immense and required checking two or three times a day. On top of all this, the ride was never really very popular and was removed at the end of the 1980 season.

A small zoo was also installed inside the former cinema, adjacent to the Ark. This was in an area between the auditorium and the former cinema entrance/café (by now part of John Ling's arcade). The zoo contained a range of small animals: monkeys, hamsters, rats, rabbits and a snake.

In addition to the ride concessions, Joyland now also had numerous smaller concession-aires operating: Stuart Keane's Kentucky Derby; Bob's Hot Dogs; Jim's Waffles & Ice Cream; Stuart's Bingo; Dave's Tattooists; Ear Piercing; and Jewellery Stall, with the Browns operating fewer attractions than ever. But this policy had allowed by far the biggest investment in new rides and attractions over a few short years that Joyland had ever seen in its history.

The Coronation Ark in Joyland at the start of the 1980 season. The ride was operating in the auditorium of the former Lounge Cinema, and it was not possible to erect all the rounding boards. A few weeks after this picture was taken, the original 1930s artwork was obliterated behind black paint.

Stephen Smith

On 25th May 1980, the Bridlington Free Press ran a feature on the 'new' Joyland:

"Joyland, the major Bridlington amusement centre, jealously guarding its claim to be one of the biggest privately-owned amusement centres in the country, has recently installed some major new rides in its complex which occupies a site through from Esplanade to Promenade. This has been made possible by the acquisition of the former Lounge Cinema, which has given them an additional 10,000 square feet of space."

A general view of the open yard area in 1980. A ride operator sits on the Cyclone Twist awaiting riders – the sign above says "Please Pay in Car". Behind the Twist is the Meteorite, also awaiting riders. The entrance to the arcade can be seen to the left, with the 'rock effect' theming above.

Stephen Smith

Chief engineer Ronald Walls pictured in 1980, with the Dodgems behind. Note the new Reverchon dodgem cars, which were introduced this season.

Stephen Smith

The new-look uniforms for the 1980 season. All staff got a new jacket with badge and were renamed 'engineers' instead of 'mechanics'. Pictured are 'engineers' Steve Lilly, Robert Flinders and Derek Taylor. Behind them can be seen the Ghost Train. The artwork behind survives at the time of writing at Rainbow Amusement Park, Hunstanton. Derek Taylor

To celebrate all this investment and enlargement, Browns decided to install a huge new illuminated entrance sign above the Promenade entrance to advertise Joyland's new status as a major indoor and outdoor amusement park. The sign, 50 feet long and eight feet high, was the largest illuminated sign in Bridlington and was topped off with a line of flags.

When the complex opened for the 1980 season, it really was an impressive sight, dominating the Promenade, rightly reflecting Joyland's status as Bridlington's biggest privately owned visitor attraction. The opening of 'new' Joyland at the start of the 1980 season was celebrated with a free hour, in which customers could ride as many rides as they could fit into the time. The intention was to get as many people in as possible and gain maximum publicity for the new line-up. They had installed a system for counting riders as they got onto the rides. Stuart Keane explains:

> "We had to press a key and display what ride number it was and how many riders were on. They had to stop the Ark once, because there were 195 people on it!"

In 1980, Browns decided that it was time to launch Joyland's first ever television advert. This was believed to be the first time an amusement arcade was advertised on British television, and was

This advert from Bridlington's 1980 Holiday Guide shows the range of attractions on offer at the complex for its most ambitious season yet. Nick Laister Collection.

partly due to the number of concessionaires within the complex. The Browns carefully graphed visitor numbers against the times when the TV advert was showing, and it showed that takings went up when the TV advert was shown.

In that big season of 1980, Joyland was a lively place, with the hits of the day echoing across the complex and the rides often operating full. It was a sight to behold. To add to the fairground atmosphere, ride operators would employ all the old travelling funfair tricks to excite the punters. The operator of the Cyclone Twist would often be heard saying: "Just one or two more people, one or two more riders, and away we go." Once the ride had started, he would carefully build up the anticipation by saying, "Do you want it faster?" to which everyone would shout: "Yes!" Then: "Do you want it slower?" to which the riders would invariably shout: "No". The operator would then reply: "Then scream – the louder you scream, the faster we go!" Of course, all the riders did, and he would slowly crank up the speed. At night, Joyland would be a blaze of coloured lights, both inside and out, a beacon throughout the town centre and seafront. The atmosphere in Joyland spilled out across that part of the town, being almost palpable.

In the 1980 season, Joyland introduced 'Carnival Nights' on Friday, with staff wearing fancy dress, and as many consecutive rides as you like for the price of one. Stuart Keane tells the story of the first Carnival Night, which included his very own illusion show:

"We did this illusion show, and I was billed as 'The Great Stuarta'. Nobody knew it was going to be me. There were bills all over the town promoting 'The Great Stuarta' It was supposed to start at eight o'clock. To get the staff into the spirit of things we got them to dress up in fancy dress, and they got £10 or £15. We got the public to judge them. First we did the illusion and then we did the Parade of the Staff."

"We did the illusion on the Speedway steps. I remember in particular the first night, the thing of the act was that I would dress up in a cowboy outfit: Stetson hat, guns, proper cowboy boots on. We got the girl in the box and did the speech, you know: 'We are going to make her disappear before your very eyes. Look; there she goes, up into the sky.' Then we get her back, and when she comes back she has only got her pants and bra on. Like we haven't brought her

Stuart Keane (left) made a huge contribution to Joyland during the 1970s and 1980s, with the installation of several rides and games. In this 1984 photograph, he is pictured with Peter Brown's wife, Linda, and Robert Brown.

Robert Brown

A general view of the Passage, looking deep into the arcade.

Reg Spencer

back properly. So we send her back again. I was getting a bit of Dutch courage in the local pub, and my manager Ray Clarke said, 'There's loads of people there, you know, plenty of people. You'd better come.' I said, 'We'll keep them waiting another five minutes.' Anyway, at twenty past eight I knocked another drink down, and we started doing the act. The microphone lead wasn't long enough. When I went for the mic lead, and I realised I was going to pull the amplifier down, my spurs got caught in the steps on the Speedway, and I went rolling backwards. The crowd laughed and gave us a clap. They thought it was part of the act! The Great Stuarta!"

World's Fair reported on Joyland's 1980 season in its 5 July issue. Correspondent Stephen Smith wrote:

"The arcade is split into sections, each containing a certain theme of machine. One section opened last year was 'Silverland', containing many modern gaming machines as well as bingo, pintables and other games. Next to this is 'Slots of Fun', which in addition to the machines has a shooting range with targets on a replica scene. One noticeable thing about the arcade is that all the machines are modern and are constantly being updated. Walking through from Esplanade to the fairground rides, one passes through another section containing a model boat marina and this part was updated last year to higher rate machines."

The Cyclone Twist proved to be the problem of the season, continually breaking down. On one day, late in the season, a young girl and her mother were on the ride when part of it collapsed. Luckily no one was hurt, but the ride was immediately removed.

The 1980 season was a reasonable success; the Meteorite being the big hit of the year. In many ways it took the attention away from the Waltzer, which had fewer riders that year. But although the Meteorite was a big hit, Stuart Keane was a little disappointed at how the season went as a whole, especially with all the new attractions, events and promotion. But the 1980

Amusement caterers get tough. Left to right: Michael Chaperlin (Joyland bingo tenant), Shaun Corrigan, Albert Corrigan and Peter Brown protest at the Council's proposals to pedestrianise the Esplanade. Peter and Linda Brown

season was just the first phase in a much longer-term expansion plan for the complex, with the ultimate aim of the brothers being to cover over the entire complex, making it an all-weather, year-round attraction.

1981 Changes

A few changes were made to Joyland for the 1981 season. Firstly, the Speedway was removed, as it was going to form part of an Olde Time Fairground at Lightwater Valley near Ripon (now the Lightwater Valley Family Theme Park). Due to the loss of the Speedway from the cinema, a new attraction had to be installed. Stuart Keane hit upon the idea of creating a Fun House, which could incorporate the existing mini zoo. The only problem was what to do with the large opening into the cinema building. Stuart Keane remembers the difficulties they faced:

"The building was quite high, about 60 feet up to the peak. The opening of the cinema build-ing looked absolutely terrible because it was just a hole. It didn't look too bad when you had a ride in there because you were blocking it off. I had a blow-up façade made for the building. And we blew it up and we had a crane to fasten it to the apex of the building. It was fastened to

the side of the building and it looked like a circus tent. It had windows, or apertures, on it where you could see people walking across for the Hell Slide. It looked great. You just had one giant fan and blew it up every morning, and it took shape."

The concept of the Fun House was to be a 'pay once and stay as long as you like' attraction, similar to today's theme parks. The entire Lounge Cinema auditorium would be used.

The Bridlington Free Press hailed the arrival of Bridlington's latest new attraction on 16th April 1981:

"The circus is coming to Bridlington for the summer season – in the shape of the Joyland Amusements' Fun House on Promenade. A giant inflatable circus-tent frontage has been installed and general rides manager Mr Ray Clarke said it was the first of its kind in the world."

The circus entrance led to a range of equipment inside the Fun House: climbing frames, playground equipment, machines and the aforementioned mini zoo. The Zoo, which was located in what would have been part of the cinema foyer, was up a flight of stairs from the main Fun House area. The staircase and landing were still highly ornate, virtually untouched from its years as a cinema. On show in the zoo for the 1981 season were monkeys, parrots, gerbils and guinea pigs. But the most popular attraction in the Fun House was the 'Hell Slide', which was a vertical slide made from wood, the 'loading station' being on a balcony immediately behind the big top frontage, so that Joyland visitors could see those in the Fun House enjoying themselves. But for many, part of the joy of visiting the Fun House was exploring the cinema building.

Stuart Keane also bought the Dodgems and Ghost Train from the Browns, and operated them in the same way as the rest of his attractions. By this time, John Ling had opened Dodgems in his arcade, and there were Dodgems on the seafront in Corrigan's small amusement park, so the Joyland Dodgems now had serious competition.

John Ling's Dodgems. Located at the rear of the arcade, these Dodgems competed with those in the centre of Joyland. The Dodgems have now been replaced with ten-pin bowling, again competing with a similar attraction in Joyland!
Michael Smith

South Cliff Amusements as it appeared throughout the 1970s. This photograph was taken in 1980, just days before its new entrance sign was installed. Geoff Gibson

This photograph was taken days after the previous one following the installation of the new illuminated sign. Geoff Gibson

Inside South Cliff Amusements in the 1980s. Inside was a mix of fruit machines, video games and novelties. Note the painted Bridlington scenes around the walls, featuring the Harbour and Flamborough Head. Geoff Gibson

Another photograph of the interior of South Cliff Amusements. Behind the one-arm bandits can be seen the Atari 'Pole Position' racing videogame. This was one of the most successful videogames of the 1980s. Geoff Gibson

Keane decided to remove the fake rock/stonework effect from around the Dodgems, which had been a feature of Joyland for almost 20 years. He boxed in all the supports to give the central part of the complex a more modern appearance, and painted the supports black.

The Meteorite was moved into the position vacated by the Twist. The former site of the Meteorite was filled with fairground games, including darts and basketball. Stuart Keane replaced the Twist with a Jackson juvenile roundabout, which he bought from showman Alf Waddington at Belle Vue Amusement Park in Manchester. The Ghost Train, Waltzer and Dodgems remained in the same locations.

In fact, by the time of the 1981 season, Stuart Keane controlled all of the major rides and attractions in Joyland.

A new system of tokens was introduced. A token booth was installed in the centre of the amusement park area, from which you could buy any number of tokens for the rides. From that point on, no cash was accepted on any of Joyland's rides. Joyland was one of the first places to introduce such a system, which has since been brought in at most of the UK's seaside amusement parks, including Blackpool Pleasure Beach, and Bridlington's current seafront rides.

Other Arcades

By the 1980s, most arcades were well established and there were few new ones opening. Bridlington still had the outward appearance of a bustling, prosperous seaside resort, but things would change as the decade progressed. One new arcade that did open in this period was the Royal Mint on Garrison Street. It opened in 1981, but its name was changed to just 'The Mint' as the use of 'Royal' in the name was too sensitive for the Registrar of Business Names. Operated by the Walker amusement family, the arcade was eventually taken over by 'The Major', a kindly ex-RAF gent with prerequisite handlebar moustache and swept-back silver hair.

Slow Down

One thing the Brown brothers began to notice in the early 1980s was that business was slowing down. This wasn't a sudden thing; it was a gradual progression that had really started in the late 1970s. Robert Brown reflects that it was not unique to Joyland – sadly it was happening throughout Bridlington:

> "With the advent of all the other arcades, package holidays, theme parks, and places in York like the Jorvik Centre and Railway Museum, our business noticeably started to go down. The business peaked from the late 1930s/early 1940s through to the mid-1960s."

In 1982, looking back over the past ten years, Peter and Robert could see there was a continuing decline. They could see no reason why this decline would stop and they began to question whether they should continue. But it wasn't just the gradual decline of the business, which was still very profitable, that got them thinking about selling. It was their relationship. Despite the outward appearance of calm and understanding, the two brothers were not getting on as well as they once had. This made their time at Joyland over the last few years less happy than it should have been.

The sci-fi appearance of Shaw's Premier Amusements in Cliff Street has been largely unchanged since the mid-1960s. Premier was the first permanent amusement arcade in Bridlington town centre. This picture was taken in 2006. Nick Laister

Close-up of the colourful frontage of Premier Amusements.

Nick Laister

The big decision to sell the business came quite suddenly, and it was taken over lunch at a trade show at the Birmingham NEC. It was Peter who asked the question that he knew they had both been thinking:

"Do you think we ought to perhaps split?" he asked.

Robert smiled at Peter and nodded knowingly. There was complete agreement between the brothers. They were to sell Joyland!

After returning from the show, they then began to discuss how they would split the business. Both decided they wanted to stay in the trade, but neither wanted to continue to operate a concern the size of Joyland. They therefore came to the decision to sell most of Joyland, but to retain small, self-contained arcades, independent from each other, at opposite ends of the complex. Peter would take Little Joyland on Esplanade, where their grandmother had started Joyland almost 50 years ago. Robert would create a similarly sized arcade on the Promenade end, by putting a partition wall down the centre of the entrance building. The remainder of Joyland, which would have smaller entrances at each end, and the entire central area, including the former Lounge Cinema and funfair, would be sold.

The obvious person to buy the remainder of Joyland was Stuart Keane. After all, he operated all the rides, so was effectively already running most of the central part of the complex. They both approached Stuart to put the idea to him, and they got a very enthusiastic response. Keane was out of the country at the time, with his attractions being managed by Ray Clarke, and he assumed that when the Browns eventually sold it, the centre of Joyland would be his.

Then, quite out of the blue, John Noble, who had bought Pleasureland from the Brown family four years earlier, found out they were planning to sell. He saw Joyland as having great long-term potential to develop into a major covered leisure complex. He knew he had to have it, and made the Brown brothers an offer which Robert Brown describes as "one we could not refuse".

The news stunned Stuart Keane:

"It was a shock to me, because it came so out of the blue. The long-term deal that we were talking about was that I'd take over the centre bit. They phoned me and said, 'We're selling Joyland, and we've agreed.' That was the first I knew of it. It went through the next day and that was it."

The Bridlington Free Press reported this change to one of the town's longest-established attractions on 8th April 1982, noting that major changes were planned by the new owners:

"The major part of the Joyland Amusement Arcade complex in Bridlington town centre, one of the biggest of its kind in Britain, has been sold to John Noble and Company in a multi-thousand pound deal…Both the brothers and Mr Noble, whose headquarters are at Chester-le-Street, are planning a new concept in entertainment – new and bigger machines, plus carpeting, and a walk-round area for families. The work will be carried out when the present season ends, but meanwhile walls have been built to divide the Browns' property from the John Noble business."

Peter Brown's arcade adjacent to Joyland's Esplanade entrance was to be called 'Slots-a-Fun'. Robert Brown's amusement centre on the Promenade side of the complex was to be called 'Starburst'.

TEN

John Noble and Sons: Joyland Shrinks, Joyland Grows

"The miner's strike was another killer. We used to depend a lot on the miners. They were very good for business. And then Butlin's at Filey (between Bridlington and Scarborough) closed. People used to go to Butlin's and they'd say, 'we'll go to Brid for a day' or 'we'll go to Scarborough'. They used to turn left or right outside of Butlin's. All these things affected us."

ROBERT BROWN

In addition to Joyland/The Forum and Pleasureland, the Nobles operate a number of other arcades in Bridlington, including the wide fronted Leisureland, pictured here in 2000. Nick Laister

The Noble name has been associated with amusements for over 100 years. John Noble had been in the amusement business for over 30 years by the time he acquired Joyland. Based in Chester-le-Street, County Durham, his company, J. Noble & Sons Ltd, operated a number of amusement arcades in town centres in the north east of England.

In 1982, John Noble, at 47, was the proud new owner of Joyland. As a former president of the trade organisation representing travelling showpeople, The Showmen's Guild of Great Britain, he was a highly respected member of the British fairground community. His two sons, 23-year-old John Jnr, his eldest son, and Jason, 16, had left school and were also now starting to contribute to the business. John also had two daughters, Dawn and Gail, who were beginning to get involved in the business.

John Noble's approach was to turn seaside amusement arcades from draughty, open fronted, concrete floored buildings to stylish, all weather attractions, influenced by the luxurious casinos of Las Vegas. This was an approach he was already successfully using in his town centre arcades. He was much-liked within the industry, not only for his undoubted business success, but also because he was a true gentleman, and a very straightforward man. Joyland was in good hands.

By the time of Joyland's acquisition, John Noble owned several other arcades in Bridlington: in addition to Pleasureland they had also taken over two relatively new arcades, Funland and Leisureland, both on Garrison Street.

All Change

Immediately following the acquisition, plans were submitted to the Council jointly by Peter and Robert Brown and John Noble in April 1982 to make the necessary alterations to both entrances to the complex. These alterations would create the two self-contained arcades for Peter and Robert. A new fascia was to be constructed across the Promenade frontage, which would see the removal of the extravagant 1980 'funfair/amusements' fascia erected by Peter and Robert Brown. New doors were to be inserted along the frontage with the 'J. Noble' motif. A similar approach would also be used at the Esplanade entrance. Planning permission was granted in May 1982.

Besides the creation of these two small arcades for Peter and Robert Brown, the remainder of Joyland remained pretty much the same throughout the 1982 season. The Nobles continued to operate it as it was. In acquiring Joyland, they also inherited the Brown's business relationship with Stuart Keane, which they also continued for the first two seasons. John Noble Snr took on direct responsibility for the Waltzer, as he saw that as a central attraction, and as it was on profit share with Stuart Keane, it was worth his while to make it succeed. After all, it was taking up a lot of space in the centre of the arcade, space that could accommodate a lot of slot machines. The only noticeable changes for visitors to Joyland were the smaller entrances and the new illuminated fascia sign installed across the Esplanade frontage.

Despite the initial appearance of 'business as usual', John Noble had no intention of operating Joyland as it was. The main reason he had acquired the complex was to move it in the direction of an indoor leisure and amusement centre rather than a funfair/amusement arcade. Noble's vision of an amusement centre was very different to that of the Browns, and could already be seen at Pleasureland. His amusement centres were luxurious, carpeted venues, with sumptuous interiors; fairground rides did not really fit in with this vision. His intention was also to try and disguise the fact that Joyland had developed by the amalgama-

The Waltzer pictured in September 1982, shortly before its removal from Joyland. The arcade was now under the ownership of J Noble & Sons Ltd, who decided to remove the rides and increase the number of slot machines. The price of a ride on the Waltzer had dropped to 25p

Michael Smith

tion of numerous properties by installing suspended ceilings. Noble also wanted to have complete control of the complex, rather than having the different concessionaires that Peter and Robert Brown had introduced, and that meant that Stuart Keane's days were numbered. The decision was taken to remove all the rides from Joyland at the end of the 1983 season. As it happened, this fitted in with Stuart Keane's own plans. It was no secret that John Noble and Stuart Keane did not see eye to eye about Joyland and the way it should progress. Therefore, it was by mutual agreement that the rides would come out.

The pit that had been created to house the Waltzer in 1979 was filled using the same material that had originally been excavated, as John Noble Jnr explains:

"We kept the raised area until we took the Waltzer out. We used the rubbish from there to fill the hole. That was approximately 1984. All of the area to the east of the Waltzer was all buildings; it was all basically blocked off."

The Fun House was also closed.

The only exception was the Dodgems, which remained at Joyland for a further season. Keane rented the Dodgems, with new plates and new cars, to the Nobles. Eventually, these too were removed, after 50 years as Joyland's central attraction. The site of the Dodgems was converted into a large café area, with a small replica house constructed as the counter, and there was a large area of seating on the site of the former Dodgem track.

The Nobles needed time to plan for the expansion of the remainder of Joyland. The most difficult area, which would require the most thought, was the open yard and the former cinema building. It was impossible to carpet and roof this area in such a small space of time; this would have to be a future project. John Noble Jnr explains:

"Basically, we just partitioned it off, and forgot about the open area. We just left it until we could think about what to do with it."

The former cinema buildings then fell into disuse. And so it was that in 1983 Joyland reopened to the public as a substantially reduced attraction. Taking into account the loss of the two arcade areas at each end, operated by the Brown brothers, and the loss of the disused open yard and cinema areas, Joyland was little over half the size it had been only two years earlier.

The Sons Take Over

Soon after acquiring Joyland, John Noble fell ill. This meant that he was unable to spend much time there. In true Joyland tradition, the sons stepped in. John Jnr and Jason, spent a significant amount of their time running the arcade and planning its future development. Due to their father's ill health, John and Jason, who were only just out of their teens, virtually ran Joyland throughout much of the 1980s. John Jnr, however, spent a lot of his time up north, managing the other arcades in the Noble chain. Jason very much took charge of Joyland. Like Harry Brown before him, he lived 'over the shop'.

Jason spent so much time in Bridlington that Joyland virtually became his life, and it is to his credit that Joyland has developed and prospered over the past 20 years, at a time when tourism in Bridlington has declined. Ronald Walls, who had worked with two generations of Browns, and the Nobles, drew parallels between the Brown Brothers and the Noble Brothers:

> *"Jason is more like Robert used to be: more on the floor. Jason knew about machines, and what will take money. John is more academic like Peter was."*

Use of the Lounge/Open Yard

In 1986, after they had improved the interior of the main areas of Joyland, the Noble family turned its attention to the open yard and former Lounge Cinema building, which had been empty for the last few years. They decided that the time had come to reopen the remainder of Joyland. The first thing was to bridge the gap between the main Joyland arcade and the Cinema building, this entire area was roofed over, creating a huge space.

Most of the former open yard area was filled with slot machines as a short term solution, before they could implement their full plans for the complex. This was the second phase of the conversion of Joyland from a fairground and amusement arcade to a leisure complex. For the first time, this truly allowed Joyland to be a year-round attraction, with the entire complex opening throughout the winter of 1987.

The former cinema auditorium, acquired by Peter and Robert Brown in 1979, proved to be the most difficult part of the complex to bring back into profitable use. A series of attractions were opened here, most of which failed, partly perhaps because they were harking back to the former fairground use, which the Nobles had been trying to move away from. Attractions that came and went in this area included a new fun house, a haunted 'walk-through', bumper boats, dodgems, a snooker and pool hall, Quasar laser tag and the Garden Café.

Peter and Robert

Peter and Robert continued to operate their separate arcades in their respective parts of what was Joyland. Doug Perriss, who had been Manager of Pleasureland since the Harry Brown days, but who had stayed on to run the place when the Nobles took over, came over to be Peter's Manager in Slots-a-Fun. Doug would stay with Peter until ill health forced him to retire.

Peter and Robert both observe now that the slow drop in business that they had witnessed through the 1970s and early 1980s continued throughout the rest of the 1980s and into the 1990s. It seems that their decision to leave the business was the correct one.

What clearly happened to Bridlington and its biggest attraction, Joyland, was happening to seaside resorts all over the country. New attractions were vying for peoples' leisure time. So many changes occurred nationally through the 1980s and into the 1990s that altered these leisure patterns, and added to the decline that had started in the 1970s. New activities such as car boot sales, Sunday shopping, extended pub opening hours, all added to this gradual erosion of visitors to Joyland, Slots-a-Fun and Starburst.

Robert remembers:

"The miner's strike was another killer. We used to depend a lot on the miners. They were very good for business. And then Butlin's at Filey (between Bridlington and Scarborough) closed. People used to go to Butlin's and they'd say, 'we'll go to Brid for a day' or 'we'll go to Scarborough'. They used to turn left or right outside of Butlin's. All these things affected us."

Peter and Robert both decided to retire from the business and sell their respective arcades in 1994. Their mother, Margaret, had died in 1993 (aged 80 years), and this was the final link with

The Esplanade in 1983. Left to right: John Noble's Joyland; Peter Brown's 'Slots A Fun' arcade; and Albert Corrigan's arcade. Peter Brown's arcade, which was retained when the brothers sold Joyland in 1982, occupied the very same unit in which Charlotte Brown first opened Joyland in 1936. But major changes were just around the corner. Bridlington Library

The end for Joyland. Joyland's Promenade frontage looked very forlorn in February 1995. Robert Brown had sold his small retained arcade, Starburst (the left hand side of the Promenade entrance) to the Nobles three months before, and the signage had been removed. Joyland was about to start a new life and a new look as the Forum.

Bridlington Free Press

the old days. They both decided it was time to quit. Peter sold Slots-a-Fun arcade first, in May 1994, followed by Robert's Starburst Amusements in November 1994. They both sold their respective parts of Joyland to J. Noble & Sons, allowing the Nobles to gain full control of the entire Joyland site for the first time.

With full control of the site, the Nobles could now invest in the future of Joyland. They were about to embark on a major programme of change, the biggest since Peter and Robert Brown had expanded the complex in 1980.

The first phase of the works involved the development of a full size AMF ten-pin bowling attraction, with an adjacent bar for the 1994/95 season.

By 1995, after the Nobles took control of the entire site, Joyland featured Ten Pin Bowling, Bar, Prize Bingo, Garden Café and Snack Bar, in addition to the huge area of slot machines. But the Promenade frontage of the arcade was a shadow of its former self. All the signs, flags and lights of Brown's Joyland were long gone, leaving a standard illuminated amusement arcade canopy, and the decaying 1930s frontage. But changes were just around the corner.

Eleven

The Forum

"With over 44,000 square feet of entertainment on the ground floor alone, it is easy to see why a trip to Brid is not complete until you take a look at what we have to offer."

The Promenade frontage of The Forum in April 2000. Behind the new façade can clearly be seen Joyland's 1930s amusement park-style art deco entrance. This entrance was once illuminated and bedecked with flags; by the start of the 21st Century, it is crumbling and almost derelict. Nick Laister

Asecond phase of the site's redevelopment was the introduction of a bar/restaurant on the first floor over the Esplanade entrance, which also had a stage for use as a music venue. The drawings which accompanied the planning application for the works showed a proposal to not only open up the first floor, but to extend it out over the ground floor, which extended several metres beyond the main building. This was to involve the erection of a multi-bayed UPVC canopy over the projecting ground floor canopy.

The proposal was met with enthusiasm from the planning officer, who summed up the appearance of Esplanade in the mid 1990s:

"The first floors and above of many of the buildings along the Esplanade are desperately in need of refurbishment. These buildings form the main inward view from the seafront for visitors to Bridlington and this type of entrepreneurial approach with flair and imagination is to be welcomed."

The space had created a 'conservatory' frontage over the Esplanade entrance looking out over Bridlington Bay. As John Noble Jnr states, "We have tried to utilise everything." It was all internally designed to the highest of standards and fully carpeted.

A large advert taken out by J. Noble & Sons in the 1995 Bridlington Guide Book celebrated the end of this second phase of work, with the opening of what was named 'Bar Utopia'. It also summarised the other attractions in Joyland for the new season:

"On first entering the Centre, all the traditional seaside attractions are available, from kiddie rides and teddy bear cranes, through to our high tech video games, where up to four players can compete. Prize Bingo has been part of the entertainment provided by our family since the turn of the century, when the game was known as 'Housey Housey'. Bingo is just as popular today…Our luxury Bingo is self-contained and offers video displays for the hard of hearing.

"In the heart of the complex you will find our Ten Pin Bowling Centre, the only full-size bowling centre in town, installed by AMF craftsmen…Our Centre is fully licensed, serving drinks at your lane from the American Theme Bar and meals from the Restaurant, Garden Café or Snack Bar, making us the ideal choice for an evening out, whether a special occasion or just meeting friends.

"With over 44,000 square feet of entertainment on the ground floor alone, it is easy to see why a trip to Brid is not complete until you take a look at what we have to offer."

The building was fitted out to modern standards of comfort and technology, a far cry from the concrete-floored Joyland of previous years. To celebrate all this hard work, Nobles knew the place needed a re-launch. It was now barely recognisable as Joyland, and the Nobles believed that the time was right for a new name for the coming Millennium. For the 1997 season, the new-look Joyland was renamed 'The Forum'. Bringing to mind the Forum of Caesar in Rome, the name was tipping its hat to the world famous Caesars Palace in Las Vegas, which had influenced the Nobles in the development of their large amusement business. Caesars Palace had opened its new 'Forum Shops' development only five years earlier. The new name was also considered to be perfect for what was planned to be the focal point of the town's leisure activity, both day and night.

And the planning officer at the council was correct when he hoped that this development would act as a catalyst for similar developments on Esplanade. Since the Joyland development, several of the other buildings have introduced development on the first floor frontages, most notably the short-lived restaurant over Corrigan's amusement arcade, adjacent to Joyland. The redevelopment of Joyland by the Noble family has, over time, resulted in a complete revitalisation of this part of Bridlington's seafront.

But this was not the end of the Nobles' plan for the Joyland complex. The next phase of development was the opening of a three-screen Cinema in the former Lounge Cinema building, where films would be shown for the first time for over 35 years. The plans were announced in the 13th March 1997 issue of the Bridlington Free Press:

> *"Film-goers will be able to see top Hollywood blockbusters in Bridlington as soon as they are released when a three-screen cinema opens in the resort this summer. The cinema is currently under construction at The Forum, on Promenade, in a bid to open in good time for the summer season."*

It is ironic that, after almost two decades of trying to find a profitable use for the former Lounge Cinema building, it would be a cinema that succeeded, although the modern interior bore little resemblance to its original opulent theatre.

An advert placed by J. Noble & Sons in the 1999 Bridlington Visitors Guide summed up the range of attractions available in the Joyland buildings at the turn of the Millennium:

> *"Thrill at one of the blockbuster movies in our multiscreen cinema. Enjoy a game of tenpin bowling at Bridlington's only full-size 10 lane bowling centre. Relax in our beautiful bar and restaurant with live entertainment, giant screen showing all the top sporting events, not to mention the fantastic views of the Esplanade, bay and Flamborough Head. The kids will be kept busy with the very latest arcade games and kiddies rides while we also cater for those who*

The Forum's Esplanade entrance in 1999. The conservatory windows on the first floor are Bar Utopia. By 1999, John Ling's (left) and Corrigan's (right) had both expanded into units adjacent to Joyland, meaning that by the end of the Millennium, amusement arcades had almost completely taken over this Esplanade block. Over the next few years, things would change, with the arcades shrinking, ownerships changing and new uses introduced. Nick Laister

can't resist prize bingo. If it's a light bite you prefer try our Wimpy fast food restaurant and as an alternative to our venue bar, you will find a full range of bottled and draft beers downstairs in the American Bar."

As the millennium came to a close, the continuous programme of development instituted by the Nobles also came to a close.

Into the 21st Century

As Bridlington moved into the new millennium, most of the amusement arcades were owned by the second wave of amusement caterers that arrived predominantly in the 1960s. On Esplanade, John Ling's (formerly Raymond Gibson's Bay View) was run by his daughter, Joanne. John Ling himself died on 21 July 1999 at the age of 88. By the late 1990s, Lings had taken over several of the units between it and the Forum to create the widest of all the arcade frontages. By 2000, almost the entire Esplanade was occupied by amusement arcades.

Since 2000, other uses have started to reappear on Esplanade, suggesting that the continuous amusement arcade development that has characterised the past 70 years is now beginning to recede. The Ling arcade has now reduced in size and now includes 'Loop', a bar and restaurant on the site of the former Lounge café.

All the properties to the north of The Forum were owned by Corrigans, who by the end of the 1990s had developed a restaurant on the first floor. The restaurant was full of fairground memorabilia, and had TV screens showing footage of old rides and fairgrounds, but was ultimately unsuccessful. At the time of writing, this arcade had been broken up, with part of it being incorporated into The Forum, under the ownership of J Noble & Sons. The remaining

Above: John Lings arcade, pictured 1999. The former Esplanade entrance to the Lounge is the mock Tudor building. Immediately to the left of the Lounge building is the original Bay View, where amusements on Esplanade started. Nick Laister

Right: Pictured in 1991 inside John Ling's arcade (formerly Bay View Amusements) is this rare Dalek coin-operated ride. Made by Edwin Hall in 1967, children can sit inside the machine, which rotates whilst an 8-track tape plays Dalek sound effects.

Nick Laister

The John Ling arcade on Esplanade in 2006. The arcade had by now significantly reduced in size and frontage from its 1999 peak. The Lounge Cinema entrance building – where Lings started – had become a bar.
Nick Laister

Loop Bar in 2006. This opened in 2003 on the site of part of the John Ling arcade. The building was originally the Lounge Café and Cinema.
Nick Laister

Above: Corrigan's amusement arcade took over the unit previously occupied by Shaw's Holiday Shop (the building with the vertical stripes). In the 1990s, it expanded to include the former Riley's Trocadero Café (the part with the balcony, a first floor restaurant which did not follow the success of the Forum's first floor experiment). Nick Laister

A new kid on the block in 2006 is Wilson's Amusements. This colourful new arcade occupies part of the former Corrigan's arcade, previously Shaw's Holiday Shop. Nick Laister

October 1999: The sad sight of Bridlington's first purpose-built amusement arcade, just weeks after it closed its doors for the last time. Built in 1923, many of the building's art deco features had been lost by the 1990s, most notably with the addition of a pantile roof. The building would be demolished in 2001. Nick Laister

Left: Bridlington's first permanent amusement arcade, Fun City, in the process of being demolished in 2001 to be replaced by a block of flats. The internal signage, visible following the removal of the front of the building, is a sad reminder of happier times. Nick Laister

The site of **Fun City in 2006. The wonderful amusement arcade has been replaced by a comparatively humdrum apartment block.**
Nick Laister

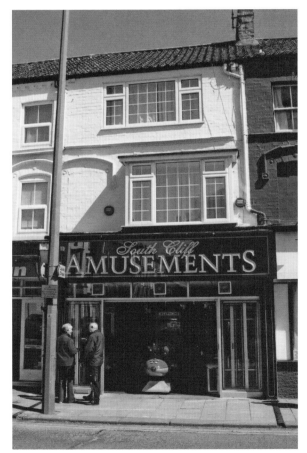

South Cliff Amusements pictured in 2006. Its new owners, J Noble & Sons Ltd, have refurbished the arcade and it now sports a new sign. Nick Laister

Chris Parcell's Old Penny Memories museum on Marlborough Terrace in 2006. The building was being advertised for sale, but Chris intends to relocate the slot machine collection on a new site. Nick Laister

Inside the Old Penny Memories slot machine museum in 1999. Located in Marlborough Terrace, the museum occupied the vacated premises of the County Club, Bridlington's private club favoured by amusement caterers.

Nick Laister

part of the Corrigan arcade is now 'Wilson's Amusements'. A new Corrigan arcade has opened on Garrison Street.

Elsewhere in the town, poor business finally resulted in the closure of Bridlington's first amusement arcade, Thompson's Fun City. It last opened in 1999 and was demolished in the summer of 2001. It has been replaced by a development of 12 flats. But Premier Amusements, Bridlington town centre's first amusement arcade, remains open.

The final connection with Bridlington's pioneering early amusement families was South Cliff Amusements, which was until recently still owned by Geoff Gibson, the son of Raymond Gibson, and the grandson of the man who first started what would later become Joyland back in the 1930s, Percy Firth. South Cliff Amusements has now been acquired by J Noble & Sons.

The County Club – the venue in which many arcade owners relaxed when their arcades had closed for the evening – was forced to close in April 1996, when membership dwindled to just 16. But it has now assumed a role fitting of its history. The building was acquired in 1995 by local businessman Chris Parcell, who has imaginatively converted it into a slot machine museum called 'Old Penny Memories'.

Old Penny Memories features a number of old slot machines of the type that would have been seen in Joyland, and is one of two slot machine museums in the town. Located in the town centre, 'Beside the Seaside' is a superbly presented, interactive museum, with a recreated vintage amusement arcade amongst its many wonderful attractions. Sadly, Bridlington's third vintage slot machine museum, 'The Vintage Toy and Train Museum', recently closed due to a change in the personal circumstances of the owner, Ian Dixon.

At the time of writing, the Forum is still owned by J Noble & Sons, and now covers a greater floor area than it has done at any time in its history, having expanded into part of the former Corrigan arcade next door (at both ground and first floor level). In addition to their recent acquisition of South Cliff Amusements, J Noble & Sons has also now acquired

Above right: Wall machines were very common in Joyland in the early years. These machines are pictured at Ian Dixon's Vintage Toy and Train Museum in 1999. Nick Laister

Above left: General view of part of the Vintage Toy and Train Museum, which featured a large collection of slot machines. The museum sadly closed in 2000. Nick Laister

Below left: Pleasureland Amusements in 2000. Formerly Southcotts tailors, it was converted into an amusement arcade by Charlotte Brown in the late 1930s. Nick Laister

Below right: Pleasureland in 2006, owned by J Noble & Sons Ltd. Nick Laister

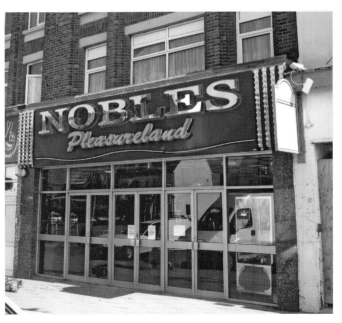

Libertys nightclub, part of the former Lounge Cinema, which is immediately adjacent to the Forum.

In March 2006, J Noble & Sons submitted plans to East Riding of Yorkshire Council for the complete redevelopment of the Esplanade frontage of the Forum, to fully integrate the adjacent Corrigan arcade into the main complex. The 1990s uPVC glazed conservatories and canopies will be replaced by a striking new glass and aluminium façade, with curved stainless steel canopy, balcony and automatic sliding doors. This will create a contemporary, unified

The former Promenade entrance to the Lounge Cinema had become 'Liberty's Discoteque' (sic) by 1999, when this photograph was taken.
Nick Laister

New investment in Pleasureland Amusements by J Noble & Sons in 2006. The entire arcade has been modernised and the premises have been expanded to include the adjacent unit on Cliff Street. As part of the building works, a bar is being constructed on the first floor.
Nick Laister

The Forum's expanded Esplanade frontage in 2006. J Noble & Sons recently acquired part of the adjacent Corrigan's arcade (the unit to the right in the picture, with temporary signage).   Nick Laister

frontage for the Forum, and will undoubtedly become a major landmark on Bridlington seafront.

It is impossible to guess in which direction the resort of Bridlington will go over the next few decades. At the time of writing, there are still plans to develop a major marina adjacent to Bridlington Harbour and the Spa complex is undergoing a multi-million pound restoration. Local businessman Michael Harrison, who has developed Bridlington's sea front amusement park over the past few years, has secured planning permission to erect a £6m, mini 'London Eye' right outside the Forum's Esplanade entrance.

Whatever the future may hold for Bridlington, the Forum will undoubtedly continue to play an important role in the town's tourism and entertainment industry, as the tangled maze of seafront buildings change and develop, assuring it remains Bridlington's centre of fun for many years to come.

TWELVE

The Rides and Attractions

Joyland has hosted a massive array of rides and attractions over the years. This section of the book takes you on a pictorial journey through some of the most memorable, and finds out the fate of many of the bigger attractions once they were removed from the arcade.

Left: The Elevenses (1955) was the most popular 'Allwin' amusement machine of all time. The trick with this game was that the long line of eleven winning cups made it look very easy. However, the steel deflectors, which can be seen just above each of the cups, meant that most balls would bounce off the pins, straight into the 'Lose' hole! Melvyn Wright

Middle: A crane machine of the type that would have appeared in Joyland. Nick Laister

Right: Oliver Whales of Redcar was one of the biggest manufacturers of automatic amusement machines. The Easy Perm was one of the most popular of the Allwins. Jonathan Plumb

An example of a typical wall mounted machine. Nick Laister

Hawtin's Clutching Hand
David Lavender

Slot machines

Allwins

These ball bearing machines were the mainstay of most amusement arcades through the middle part of the last century, and dominated Joyland for many years. A ball bearing is shot around a track by a trigger towards a series of losing and winning cups. The format known as the 'Allwin' became the classic gaming machine that was in production by many makers for over 50 years.

Many of the Joyland Allwins were made by Oliver Whales of Redcar and by Frank Hawtin, who was a dentist in Blackpool.

Cranes

These machines worked on the illusion that there would be a good prize for minimal outlay. All the customer was required to do was steer a hooking device and grab a prize. The machines often had scenes such as docks or steelworks; anywhere where a crane would be appropriate. During the War, Joyland's cranes became unusable as there was a shortage of prizes to put in them.

The Clutching Hand

This was very popular in Joyland, and was a variation on the crane theme. This machine was devised by Frank Hawtin in 1938 and, instead of a normal crane, the grab mechanism was an articulated model of the human arm and hand. The hand was used to try and pick prizes from a rotating table. Each hand had a rubber grip, which was eventually removed by the Browns because they were picking up too many prizes. Many visitors to Joyland just before, during or after the War remember this machine fondly. Examples of this machine survived in Joyland and Pleasureland until 1978.

Rotaries

Another popular prize-winning device was the Rotary. The Rotary was a glass table with four arms on it and what looked like napkin rings underneath the base. The arm moved across the table and the player could control it up to a point, after which the machine took over. In Joyland, it was, for many years, Peter Brown's job to fill up the rotaries with toys. He would walk around Joyland with a basket, similar to a supermarket basket, full of imitation diamond rings, brooches and earrings. Customers regularly complained they never won anything from these machines, yet they required refilling four times a day!

Pushers

These machines worked on a simple, but effective, concept: customers insert coins, which drop onto a flat surface and push the existing pile of coins – which are precariously hanging over the edge of a flat area – closer to the edge. Eventually they fall down a payout chute into the customers hands. However, most of the coins fell down a chute to each side of the flat surface, into the machine. These machines were not introduced into Joyland until the mid-1960s, when Sid Brown ordered his first pusher, called 'Wheel-A-Win', from Crompton Machines Ltd. These machines became massively popular and Joyland, as with most other arcades in Bridlington, introduced numerous pushers throughout the 1960s and 1970s.

Several pushers still operate in the Forum to this day, and are still common in arcades up and down the country.

Fruit Machines

Fruit, or 'Reel', machines were also very popular in Joyland. An arm is pulled, which spins several reels, each with up to ten symbols on. The machine paid out for a row of matching symbols, or specific combinations. In the early days of Joyland these machines had to have attachments allowing the player to stop them at will, in other words to add an element of skill, otherwise they would have been classed as gaming machines and therefore would have been illegal at the time. It was necessary for the player to seek the win from an attendant, as they were not able to automatically pay out. This all changed in 1963, when Bally launched the 'Money Honey' fruit machine, which featured an electrical payout technique. This type of slot machine became known informally as a 'one-armed bandit' because of its appearance and its ability to leave the gamer penniless.

Rifle Range

Several rifle ranges have graced Joyland over the years. These machines feature closely spaced mechanical targets, centred some distance away from the rifle. During World War II, Joyland changed the targets to suitable heads of the enemy, most notably Hitler!

Working Models

These are some of the most fondly remembered machines in Joyland, and due to its size, Joyland had a full set. These machines were for amusement only, and offered cheap entertainment in the form of a brief animated play, in return for a penny in the slot. They were particularly popular in Joyland after World War II. The plays were often horrific in theme; Fred Bolland's 'The Burglar', 'Drunkard's Dream' and 'The Haunted Churchyard' are examples of those that featured in Joyland. Mr Bolland had an ingenious scheme: during World War II he had bought up all the apparently useless crane machine cabinets. After the War he converted them all into working models; many of Joyland's working models were once crane machines. In the 1960s, Joyland also featured the 'Haunted House', 'Crying Baby' and 'Roadworks'.

Box Ball

This was an early form of bingo. Each person playing had a wooden ball, which they would throw and try to get the correct numbers. It had to be designed in this way, as it had to be a game of skill due to the gaming laws of the time. This was a difficult game to win.

Moonraker

This was an enormous, walk-around machine. It was themed with craters on the Moon. The player inserted coins, which trickled down, and landed in the craters. When a crater eventually collapsed, the player got all the money.

The Burglar is one of the large series of 'Working Models', popular in arcades in the Second World War. This machine is pictured at the Vintage Toy and Train Museum, Bridlington.

Nick Laister

The Guillotine.

The Laughing Sailor became synonymous with Joyland over many years, operating by its Promenade entrance. This machine was at the Vintage Toy and Train Museum in 1999. Nick Laister

The 'Cry Baby' working model.

Greyhound Derby

This was another massive machine, which the Browns had made with 'Chebs Lad', Harry Brown's racehorse, written onto it.

Laughing Sailor

The Laughing Sailor was a popular attraction at Joyland for many years. The customer would put his or her money in the slot, and the sailor would laugh infectiously, whilst swaying back and forth.

The sailor's laughing track was an old vinyl 78 record. Each summer, Joyland's mechanics had to unscrew the arm and move it along the record because the record went grey, so each year it would play a little portion of the record. This would be done each year until the hole in the middle was reached, after which the record would be turned over, moving it along the opposite side. Eventually, when the record ran out, Browns replaced it with a tape, as the records were no longer available.

This was a simple attraction that became something of a trademark for Joyland over the years due to its location just outside the Promenade entrance. At the opposite side of the entrance was a similar machine called the 'Cry Baby'. The only difference being, instead of paying to hear a machine laugh, you paid to hear it cry. The Chemist at the opposite side of the Promenade often came across and said: "Could you turn it down a bit? It is driving me mad! I'm trying to sort the tablets out and that thing's crying all the time!"

Boneo

Another popular attraction, and one that replaced the Cry Baby by the Promenade entrance in the 1970s, was Boneo, a latex skeleton inside a coffin which sang the song 'Them Bones Theme Bones', whilst dancing around its coffin.

The rides

Joyland featured fairground rides almost from the very start, and for many it is the rides that provide the strongest memories. This aspect of the complex was developed and expanded through the years, peaking in the early 1980s. In this trip down memory lane, we tell the story of some of Joyland's major rides, including where they were before they came to Joyland, and where they went when they left.

The Dodgems

The Joyland Dodgem track survived for over 50 years. It had been rebuilt in the late 1930s by Charlotte Brown, to replace the earlier (and smaller) track installed by Percy Firth. The cars were built by Supercar of Coventry.

The original cars from the 1930s were still being used in the 1970s. The cars were extremely heavy and took two men to lift them onto their sides. One daily task was to sweep the Dodgem track with long brushes – four men abreast – to get up the graphite (graphite is sprinkled on the floor to decrease friction).

In 1981, the Dodgem track was getting into a poor condition. It was well over 40 years old at this time, and the attendants would jokingly announce it on the microphone as "the only

Dodgem track with more hills than the Himalayas!" This was due to the plates rolling up in the middle. It was this requirement for maintenance that was behind Stuart Keane's decision to buy the ride from Browns, refurbish it, put on some new cars and get the plates sorted out. The old Supercar Dodgems were replaced with newer Reverchon cars with token boxes for the 1980 season.

When Stuart Keane pulled out of Joyland at the end of the 1982 season, the Dodgems remained for a further year, and were rented from Keane by the Nobles.

When the ride was removed at the end of the 1983 season, it was in excellent condition. The cars, which were still nearly new, were sold to Keith Emmett at Milton Keynes. The track was a permanent fixture in the building, so had to be scrapped. The upper section of the Dodgem track still survives over the ten-pin bowling.

Ghost Train 1

This ride was Joyland's first ghost train, and was built in the open yard, opposite the Dodgems. It was of wooden construction, with six cars, and was of permanent (as opposed to travelling) construction. It was installed in the mid-1930s by Percy Firth, but continued to be operated by the Browns in their much-expanded amusement park.

It was removed in the winter of 1951/52, to make way for the Chariot Racer. The cars, track and effects were in very poor condition and are believed to have been scrapped as they were not considered to be in a suitable condition to sell on.

Them Bones Them Bones: Joyland's all signing and dancing skeleton, Boneo, pictured in the early 1970s in the Workshop. Steve Honour is re-wiring the machine.
Ronald Walls

Chariot Racer

This ride was approximately 40 feet in diameter. It was built by Orton & Spooner as an Autodrome, which was new to Edwin Corrigan in 1939 (an autodrome is similar to a waltzer or an ark, but has fixed cars in the shape of large pre-war sports cars instead of animals or spinning cars). It was installed over the winter of 1951-52. Corrigan had converted it to an Ark before its sale to Joyland. The ride had 24 horses, with 6 chariots and could carry up to 50 passengers in one ride. It was driven by 4 DC motors and a generator. Although advertised for sale in 1953, the ride remained in Joyland through the 1950s and 1960s.

At the end of each summer the ride was pulled down, and stored on the Dodgem track.

The ride was removed in 1972, when the Brown brothers installed a new Ghost Train, and was sold back to Corrigans, who took it to Marvel's Amusement Park at Scalby Mills, Scarborough, where it operated as a Speedway. In 1975, it left Scarborough and operated at Rhyl and Skegness, before it was finally scrapped at the end of the decade.

Ghost Train 2

This was bought new from Supercar by Peter and Robert Brown in the early 1970s.

The ride was installed in the open yard, opposite the Dodgems, then moved for the 1980 season when the Browns purchased the Lounge Cinema.

It was a large Ghost Train, giving a substantial ride. The ride was entirely on one level; the cars entered via two sets of double doors, the second of which triggered a siren. The ride was powered by a generator, which was kept at the back of the pinball alley, in the Promenade end of the arcade. When the ride was moved in 1980, onto the site of the Lounge Cinema projec-

The distinctive artwork on the Ghost Train was still intact in the ride's new home of Hunstanton in 2000.
David Wragg

The former Joyland Ghost Train today at Rainbow Amusement Park, Hunstanton. The exterior of the ride has now been partially repainted, removing much of its original Joyland artwork. Keith Hamilton

tion room, it was too far away from the generators, so Peter and Robert Brown acquired a rectifier for it.

It operated in its new position from 1980 to 1982, after which it was removed from Joyland when Stuart Keane pulled out (Keane had acquired the ride from Browns in 1981). Keane moved the Ghost Train onto the seafront and operated it in Corrigan's amusement park. The ride was not easily moved as it was not designed as a travelling ride. The Ghost Train operated for one season (1983) on Bridlington seafront before it was sold to Frederick Pooley, who operated rides at Rainbow Amusement Park in Hunstanton, the popular Norfolk seaside resort. The ride still operates at Hunstanton.

The ex-Joyland Ghost Train operating at Hunstanton in June 2000. The cars are still the Joyland originals. Nick Laister

Waltzer

The Waltzer is one of the most popular rides to appear in British fairgrounds and first appeared in 1933. Joyland's nine-car Waltzer was new in 1979 from Waltzer manufacturer Jackson's of Congleton.

The Joyland Waltzer was unique as it was inside a building and riders had to go down steps to get to it. It was believed to be the only waltzer with this feature.

When the ride first opened it was a major hit. It took a small fortune in money for the Browns and Stuart Keane that first season. The novelty of a ride inside a building, and down in a hole, made it a major hit for Joyland and Bridlington and a large number of fairground enthusiasts came to Bridlington to see it. The combination of its location, the lights, and the loud music, also made it a much talked about attraction, and it became a focal point for the complex.

Unfortunately, the ride was not able to sustain its initial popularity. Whether this was because other new rides in Joyland installed after the Waltzer stole the limelight, or just that the nov-

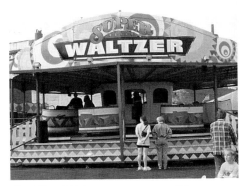

The Disco Waltzer was removed from Joyland in 1982 and then operated on the seafront in Corrigan's Amusement Park. This photograph shows the ride in 1993.

Clive Briggs

The ex-Joyland waltzer operating at the Metroland indoor theme park at Gateshead in 2000. The ride was again operating indoors, as at Joyland, and was now called 'The Whirling Waltzer'. Operated initially by Stuart Keane, who owned the ride when it was at Joyland, the centre paybox had been removed and the ride extensively themed. Nick Laister

elty had worn off, is not known. But after that first year, the takings of the ride gradually declined, never to levels where it would have forced its removal, but it never again matched the popularity of its first season. The price of the ride was reduced in later years in an attempt to boost the number of riders.

The reason for the ride's removal was not its declining popularity, but the change in ownership. It was finally removed from Joyland in 1982 when Stuart Keane left the complex. The ride was moved, with the Ghost Train, onto the seafront, into Albert Corrigan's amusement park. Eventually, in 1984, Keane sold the Waltzer to Albert Corrigan. Corrigan operated the ride for 14 years (in 1995, it operated as a Speedway, with motorbikes instead of waltzer cars). In 1998, it was bought back by Stuart Keane who refurbished it and then operated it for several years at Metroland in Gateshead's Metro Centre. The ride is now owned by Arlington Leisure and still operates at Metroland.

Meteorite

The Meteorite was new in 1980 from Sam Ward. It was a new style of machine, trailer mounted, and included novel automatic features, such as self-positioning of openings and air operated doors. The paybox contained all the controls, and allows the controller to view the ride while up and when loading.

At the end of the 1982 season, Keane removed the Meteorite from Joyland and operated it at Flamingo Land, a large zoo near Malton. In 1983, it was acquired by travelling showman John Stuart Brixton, who still operates it in the south of England. It still carries the unique motif 'Dare to be Scared' over the paybox.

Only one year after leaving Joyland, the Meteorite was travelling the fair circuit in the south of England under the ownership of John Stuart Brixton. This photograph was taken at the Beaconsfield May Fair in 1983. Michael Smith

The Speedway

The Speedway was acquired from Walter Shufflebottom, the owner of Clarence Pier amusement park in Southsea. When originally acquired, the ride was still in its special décor for the 1953 Coronation. As the centre truck was still on solid-tyre wheels, it was low-loaded up from Southsea to Bridlington, and the rest of the machine was brought up in two containers. The ride was located in the former Lounge Cinema auditorium, which was acquired by Joyland towards the end of 1979.

The ride was removed from Joyland at the end of the 1980 season, as it was destined for an Olde Time Fairground at Lightwater Valley, near Ripon, for which Stuart Keane was going to provide some of the attractions.

After leaving Joyland, it had to be put into storage. Stuart Keane tried to resist the ride being separated. There were large numbers of people wanting to buy the decoration, the rounding boards, etc, but no takers for the entire ride.

In 1996, independent showman Jack Schofield, owner of a set of gallopers which he travels around the rallies of the East Midlands, had become interested in tracking down the legendary Coronation Ark. With the help of teacher and fairground enthusiast Stephen Smith they managed to get in touch with Stuart Keane, who they met at the Hilton Hotel in York. He took them both in his Mercedes to a mill at Sowerby Bridge near York. Here they found the mounts, flash, pillars and handrails. The rest of the ride was stored at a farm near Kirby Misperton in North Yorkshire.

Schofield and Smith arranged for the remainder of the ride (the centre) to be moved from the barn to Schofield's yard at Retford in Nottinghamshire. As the ride was stored on the upper floor of the barn it all had to be removed by hand into a trailer.

As Stephen Smith remembers:

"Bright paintwork was mostly covered with a matt black although one or two pieces had somehow escaped the unskilled transformation of what was once the 'Cavalcade of Thrills' on Southsea's famous Clarence Pier. Although some rounding boards had succumbed to the dark gloom of the 'new' paint, some, including the extension front, still bore those cartoon cameos

The Coronation Ark pictured at Southsea's Clarence Pier Amusement Park in 1974. This ride would open in the auditorium of the former Lounge Cinema as part of the expanded Joyland complex in 1980. The original artwork would be painted black. Michael Smith

Close-up of the motorbikes on the Coronation Ark at Southsea.
Michael Smith

The former Joyland Twist operating at a steam rally in July 2000, under the ownership of the Dorman Brothers. The ride operated at Joyland for the 1980 season only.

David Wragg

of Britain at War. The portraits of a young looking Queen Elizabeth and her consort had also survived intact, but a decision had to be made: was what was left worth saving? Since the loss of the sister machine to Canada in 1975 this was the only survivor of the pair which left Lakin's works in May 1937."

The ride is now stored in Jack Schofield's yard, awaiting potential restoration in the future.

Cyclone Twist

Joyland's short-lived Twist was a 'grasscutter' style ride called the Cyclone Twist and was built by Church Engineering in 1978 for showman Monty Hammond.

Twist rides have been operating in the United Kingdom since the early 1960s, and are heavily influenced by American rides of the post-war period. In addition to imported models, UK-based manufacturers such as Bennett, Edwin Hall and Pollard made them. The 'grasscutter' design, such as the Joyland Twist, flew close to the ground, with nothing between the passengers' feet and the concrete base. Other twists used a platform with wheels.

The Twist was bought by Stuart Keane from Monty Hammond in 1980, and was in a poor state of repair (which is surprising considering it was only two years old). Robert Brown had accompanied Stuart Keane when he bought it and agreed that it was a bit of a mess, but they believed they could renovate it and it would make a positive addition to Joyland's expanding range of fairground rides.

Following the incident in which the ride collapsed in service, it was packed up and moved to a yard in the Old Town. It was then put in storage with the Speedway at a barn near Kirby Misperton. When Jack Schofield and Stephen Smith collected the former Joyland Speedway from the barn, the Twist came with it as the farmer insisted that if they wanted the Speedway they must take the Twist as well. The Twist was sold on to non-Guild showmen the Dorman Brothers, who restored and completely rebuilt the ride and now operate it alongside their vintage (1933) Dodgems at rallies in the East Midlands.

The final word goes to Stuart Keane, who sums up Joyland's experience with the Twist: "It was a bad ride; we should never have bought it."

About the author

Nick Laister is an Oxfordshire-based planning consultant and a leading authority on the UK tourism industry. He is a Chartered Town Planner and Planning Director with RPS, the UK's largest planning consultancy, and specialises in planning for visitor attractions and major mixed use development. He is involved in the promotion of development projects around the UK and Ireland, and has appeared as expert witness at several public inquiries and hearings. He is regularly interviewed on television and radio about visitor attractions and has written articles for numerous newspapers and journals on the same subject. He has been invited to speak at a number of conferences on the subject of planning for tourism and leisure. He also leads a campaign to save Dreamland, a historic amusement park in Margate, UK.

Like many Yorkshire-born people, Nick spent many childhood summers in Bridlington, which is when he fell in love with the town and its various attractions. Nick still visits Bridlington on holidays with his own family, and retains a fondness for the resort that played such a major role in the development of the family amusement arcade.

Further Reading

The Bridlington Book by Bryan Waites. Highgate Publications (Beverley) Ltd, 1988.
Arcades and Slot Machines by Paul Braithwaite. Carters Books, 1997.
Amusement Machines by Lynn F. Pearson. Shire Publications Ltd, 1992.
Ninety Years of Cinema in Bridlington, Brian Horney, 1995
Seaside Architecture by Kenneth Lindley. Hugh Evelyn, 1973
The People's Palaces, by Lynn F. Pearson. Barracuda Books, 1991
Bridlington: An Introduction to its History and Buildings by David and Susan Neave. Smith Settle Ltd, 2000
Port, Resort and Market Town: A History of Bridlington by David Neave. Hull Academic Press, 2000
Live Like a Lord: James Corrigan's Batley Variety Club, Bob Preedy. R E Preedy, 2002